Richard Serra

Torqued Ellipses

Dia Center for the Arts, New York

Richard Serra

Torqued Ellipses

Edited by Lynne Cooke and Karen Kelly

Designed by Laura Fields

Printed by Enterprise Press, New York

ISBN 0-944521-35-5

Library of Congress Catalogue Card Number 97-76918

Richard Serra: Torqued Ellipses

Dia Center for the Arts

545 West 22nd Street

September 25, 1997, through June 14, 1998

Torqued Ellipse I, 1996

Cor-Ten steel

13'1" height x 29' length x 20'7" width (28" overhang)

Torqued Ellipse II, 1996

Cor-Ten steel

12' height x 29' length x 20'5" width (58" overhang)

Double Torqued Ellipse, 1997

Cor-Ten steel

outside ellipse: 13'1" height x 33'6" length x 27'1" width (33" overhang)

inside ellipse: 13'1" height x 25'11" length x 20'11" width (25" overhang)

Table of Contents

Preface and Acknowledgments

> *What interests me is the opportunity for all of us to become something different from what we are, by constructing spaces that contribute something to the experience of who we are.*
>
> —Richard Serra

Richard Serra's highly ambitious yet generous goal has perhaps never before found more extraordinary expression than in his latest series, the Torqued Ellipses. Exceptionally in these sculptures, Serra started with the void, that is, space shapes a volume that is defined by material—here, by sheet steel which becomes "the skin of the void"—in contradistinction to much of his previous work, when he started with material as matter, as mass. The result is a body of work in which seemingly unaccountably, certainly unprecedentedly, space moves and shifts in response to the viewer's motion in and around the forms.

In the interview included in this publication, Serra describes with characteristic eloquence, limpidity, and directness the genesis of these sculptures in a visit he made some years ago to Borromini's church, San Carlo, in Rome. After subsequent research and protracted struggle, he finally created the first four in what is planned to be an extended series of large-scale works. In addition, he explores and elaborates their relations to certain of his abiding preoccupations, in particular to the way the processes of reception of the work provide both the means of apprehension and determine content.

While drawing extensively on his own conversations with the artist as well as on published statements, Mark Taylor's original and illuminating analysis is ultimately based in a philosophical reading of the central issues the work raises for him, a philosopher and professor of religion at Williams College in Williamstown, Massachusetts. Taylor subtly articulates parallels and affinities between Serra's integration of space-time in sculptures that demand a peripatetic vision and an extended temporality with the concept of *MA*, a foundational principle in all Japanese art forms that integrate the performative and the spatial. By deftly juxtaposing this with certain related concepts in recent Western philosophy, Taylor weaves a rich and nuanced theoretical frame through which to experience works indubitably and unequivocally grounded in direct sensory engagement. Many people have contributed to the realization of this remarkable installation at Dia. Our first and greatest debt is to Richard Serra, with whom it has long been our wish to make a project. To him and to Clara Weyergraf-Serra we extend our warmest thanks and appreciation.

This ambitious exhibition of Serra's Torqued Ellipses would not have taken place without contributions from many of Dia's and the artist's long-time supporters, including Constance R. Caplan, Douglas S. Cramer, Doris and Donald G. Fisher, Mimi and Peter Haas, Simone and Paulo Klabin, Wanda M. Klabin, Wynn Kramarksy, Nancy and Steven H. Oliver, Giovanna and Giuseppe Panza di Biumo, Miuccia Prada and Patrizio Bertelli, Emily Rauh Pulitzer, Leanne and George R. Roberts, Kathy and Keith Sachs, Hannelore and Rudolph Schulhof, Helen and Charles R. Schwab, Dorie and Paul Sternberg, Pat and Bill Wilson, and Virginia and Bagley Wright.

We extend special thanks to Larry Gagosian who made this publication possible. It was a great pleasure to work with Ken Goebel and Jose Mejia at Enterprise Press.

The artist joins us in thanking those who worked to realize both the sculptures and the installation, particularly Peter Costa, Allen Glatter, Trina McKeever, John Silberman, Richard Gluckman, Jim Schaeufele, Hank Jones and the crew at Beth Ship in Baltimore.

Michael Govan, Director

Lynne Cooke, Curator

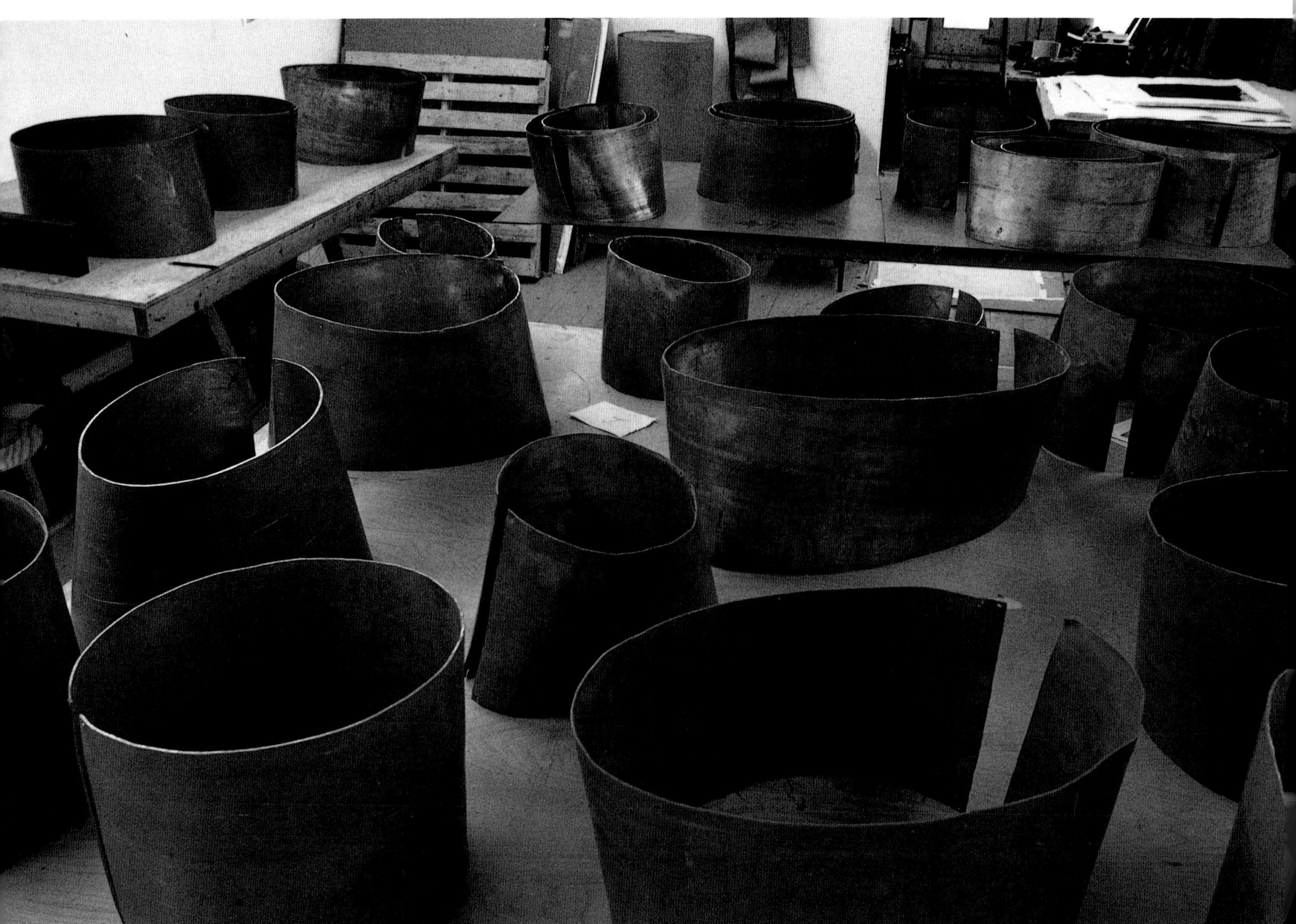

Interview with Richard Serra

Lynne Cooke and Michael Govan

Lynne Cooke: Richard, how did this new series of sculptures come about?

Richard Serra: They developed logically out of earlier pieces, such as *Olson* (1985–86) and *Intersection* (1992). *Olson* and *Intersection* consist of conical shapes whose radii differ between the top and the bottom. If you invert them and stand between them, one will lean away from you and one will lean toward you. The spaces in both sculptures are already somewhat destabilized. I wanted to build a piece that could envelop the whole space, and both lean in and out simultaneously. But, I wasn't sure if it could be done.

In the early nineties, I went to Rome, where I saw Borromini's San Carlo, which has an oval dome. And I thought it might be possible to torque that space. When I came back to New York, I tried to work it out on my bender. Since I didn't know how to cut the template to make the form, I phoned Frank Gehry's engineer, Rick Smith, who was trained in the aerospace industry, and explained my problem to him: using the same center, overlap one oval on the other oval, one ellipse on another, and rotate them in elevation. He said that it was possible in theory but that he hadn't the time to work on it with me.

With my assistant, Allen Glatter, I cut two pieces of wood and nailed a dowel between them, so that one was at a right angle to the other. Then we laid a sheet of lead on the floor and wrapped the lead around the wheels. Since the ovals are at right angles to each other, the wheels rolled in an S-like curve. That double S-curve delineated the template necessary to make the shape. If you think of how the back wheels of a broken tricycle will form lines on the ground, you can easily imagine how it functions.

After we unfurled and reduced the template, we sent it back to Rick Smith, who said it was within millimeters of what he would have come up with. Once we had given him the coordinates of the major and minor axes, and told him how we wanted to rotate the angles, he provided us with a CATIA program that determined the lines of the bending patterns according to which the actual steel templates would be rolled.

Because these forms aren't conical, the radius doesn't change in elevation. Nobody in the steel industry had manufactured forms like them before. I usually work with General Dynamics, but they wouldn't touch it: they didn't have the machinery, and they thought

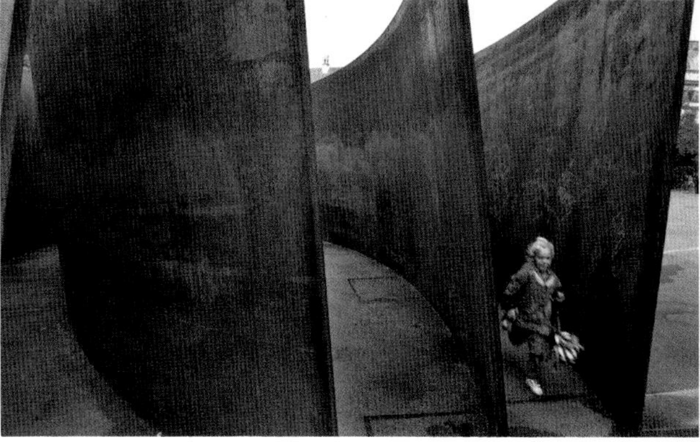

that if they attempted it, the product would not have the necessary tolerances. So I sent the computer disk with the copy of the program to every manufacturer and fabricator in the United States who I thought could handle it. No one would accept the job. Then I went to Korea. The Koreans could build it, but they don't make sixteen-foot-wide plates, they only make twelve-foot-wide plates. I went to Germany, where they have the plates, but they don't have a bender with sufficient capacity. At that point, I didn't think I would be able to make the work at all, although by then we were pretty far along in developing the models, and we were convinced that the project was worth pursuing. Also—and this is an aside—we thought that the idea could find

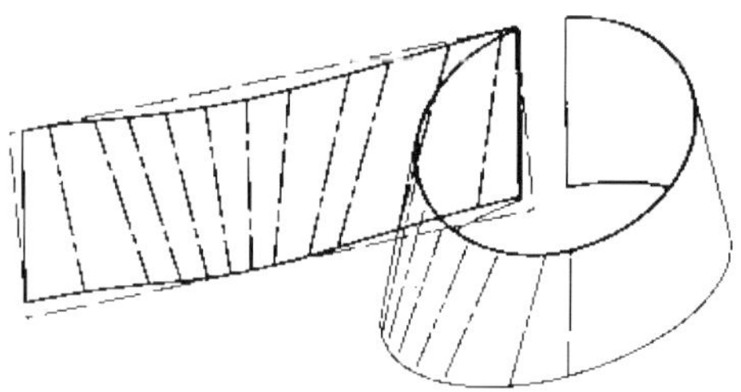

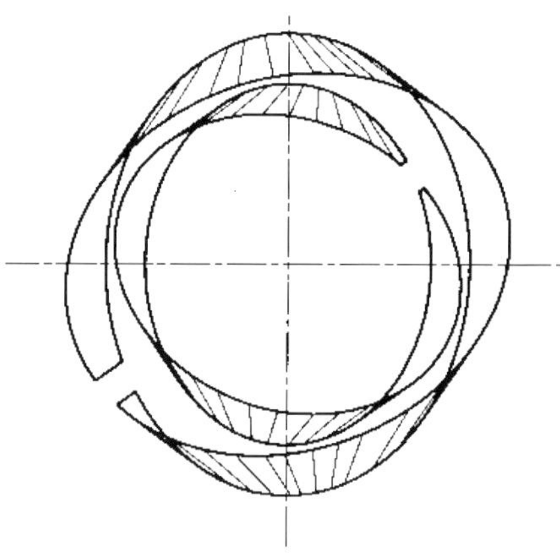

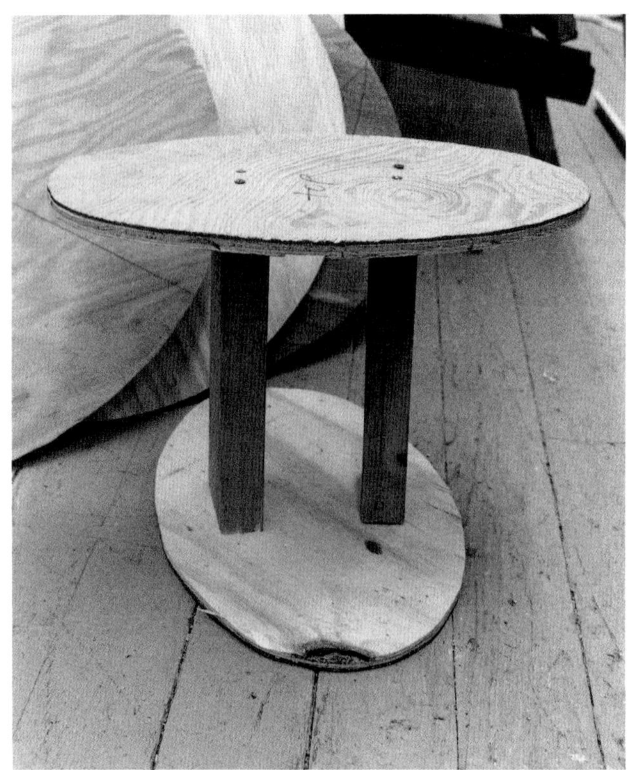

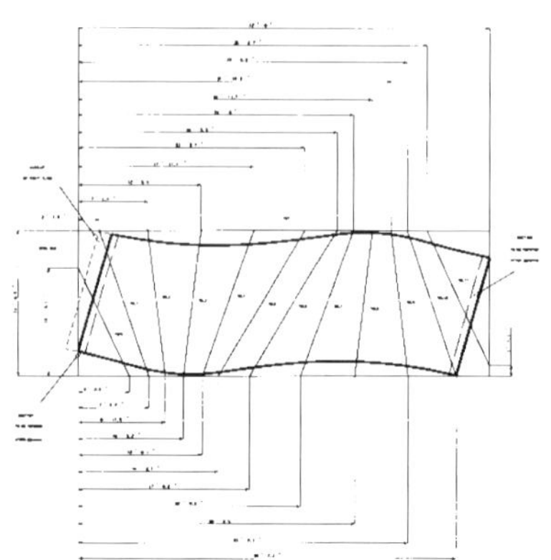

practical applications. For example, with this design you could change the flow of gas, air, or whatever, from one direction to another within a contained volume.

We finally found a place, Beth Ship, a shipyard and rolling mill in Maryland, who was interested in the problem. Their roller is constructed so that there are two small rollers below and a large roller above, which means it can open at an angle to exert more compression on one end than on the other when required. It's a large machine, between forty and fifty feet long, and it generates a tremendous amount of compression. Only four of these machines, called Hugh-Smiths, were built during the Second World War in Scotland. They were used to bend steel for battleships. I think there are only two left in existence. After going all around the country, I came to the conclusion that this was probably the only machine available that could build these pieces.

When the rolling crew at Beth Ship saw our program, they were convinced that we didn't know what we were talking about, that, in fact, these were just conical shapes inverted on themselves, and that they could be bent as they have always bent cones. Consequently, they over-bent the first shape on the first day, and broke in half a two-inch, sixteen-foot-wide, forty-foot-long plate. During the second attempt, they cracked the plate. In the end, it took a year to build the first piece. Since then, we've built three more, the last of which is an ellipse inside of an ellipse, a double ellipse. This all took maybe six months. The problem now is that the shipyard has been sold, and I'm not sure if I'm going to be able to fabricate there any longer.

When the pieces were erected on the floor, and I first walked into them, I was as startled as anyone. While working on an experimental form, I don't care about the aesthetics of the work—that seems to come after the fact, if at all. I just want to get the job done. We started with an ellipse that torqued at a fifty-five-degree angle, then we built one with a ninety-degree torque. In *Double Torqued Ellipse*, the ellipse inside the ellipse, each ellipse is torqued at seventy degrees.

I wasn't interested in the aesthetics of these pieces, but in the fact that a generic form, an ellipse, could be torqued on itself to produce a form not seen before. This form doesn't exist in architecture, nor in pottery. But once you see it, it seems quite logical. The interesting aspect for me in developing the form was that in the past, I had always started with the plate. By starting with the material, you're starting from the outside: you're constructing a space. In most of the work that preceded the Torqued Ellipses, I was forming the space in between the material that I was manipulating, and I was focused on the measure and placement of the work in relation to a given context. In these pieces, by contrast, I was starting with the void, that is, starting with the *space*, starting from the inside out, not the outside in, in order to find the skin.

I wasn't particularly concerned with what the skin looked like. The issue became how to relate the top and bottom ellipse to each other and how to rotate the void. If you place them at a right angle to each other, as in *Torqued Ellipse I*, there's no perpendicular line, no vertical section. The form continuously leans either in or out. With any relationship less than ninety degrees, there'll be four verticals within the form itself, but they aren't discernible by eye. One of the strange things about these pieces, as you follow the form from the

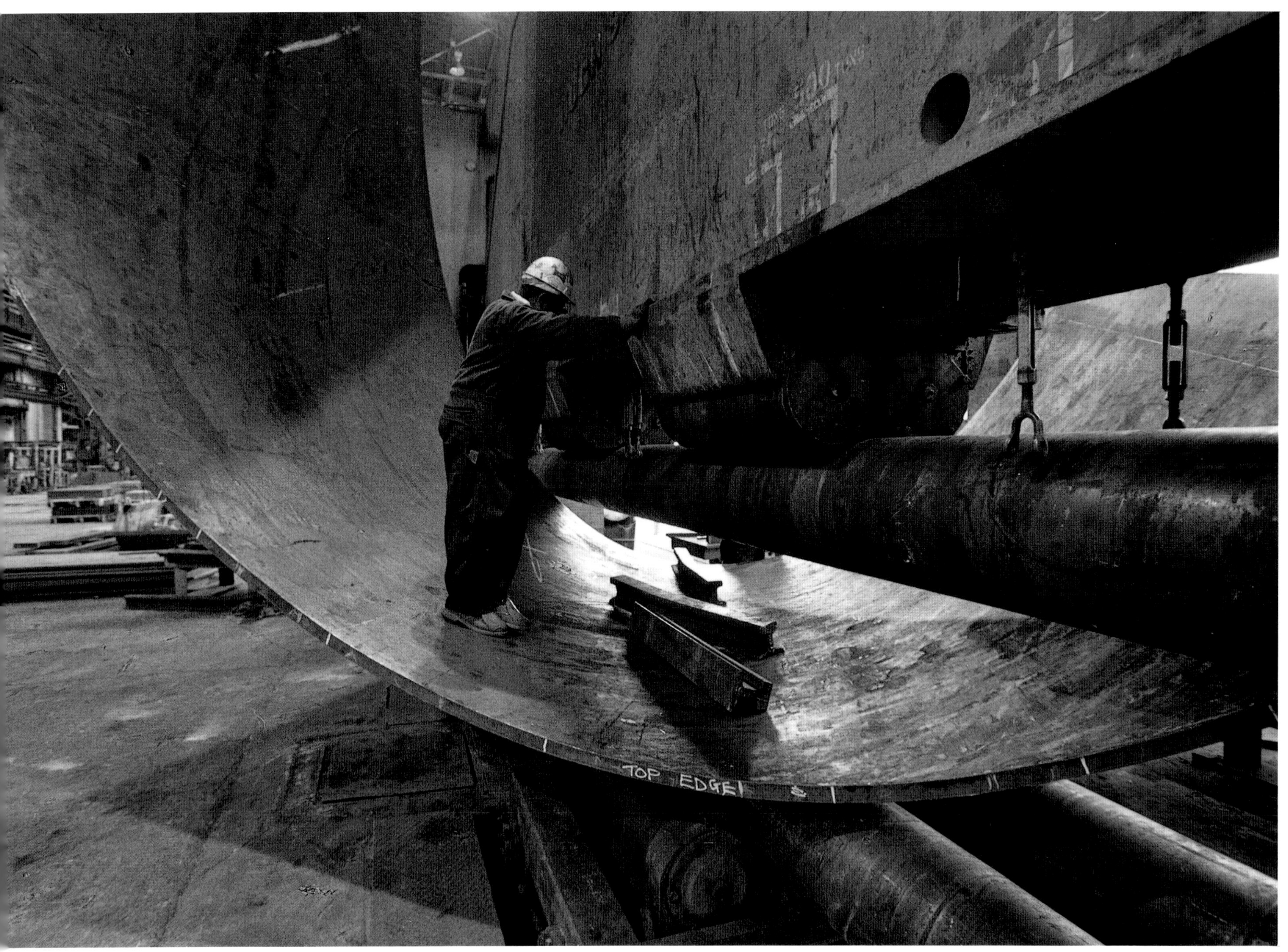
TOP EDGE

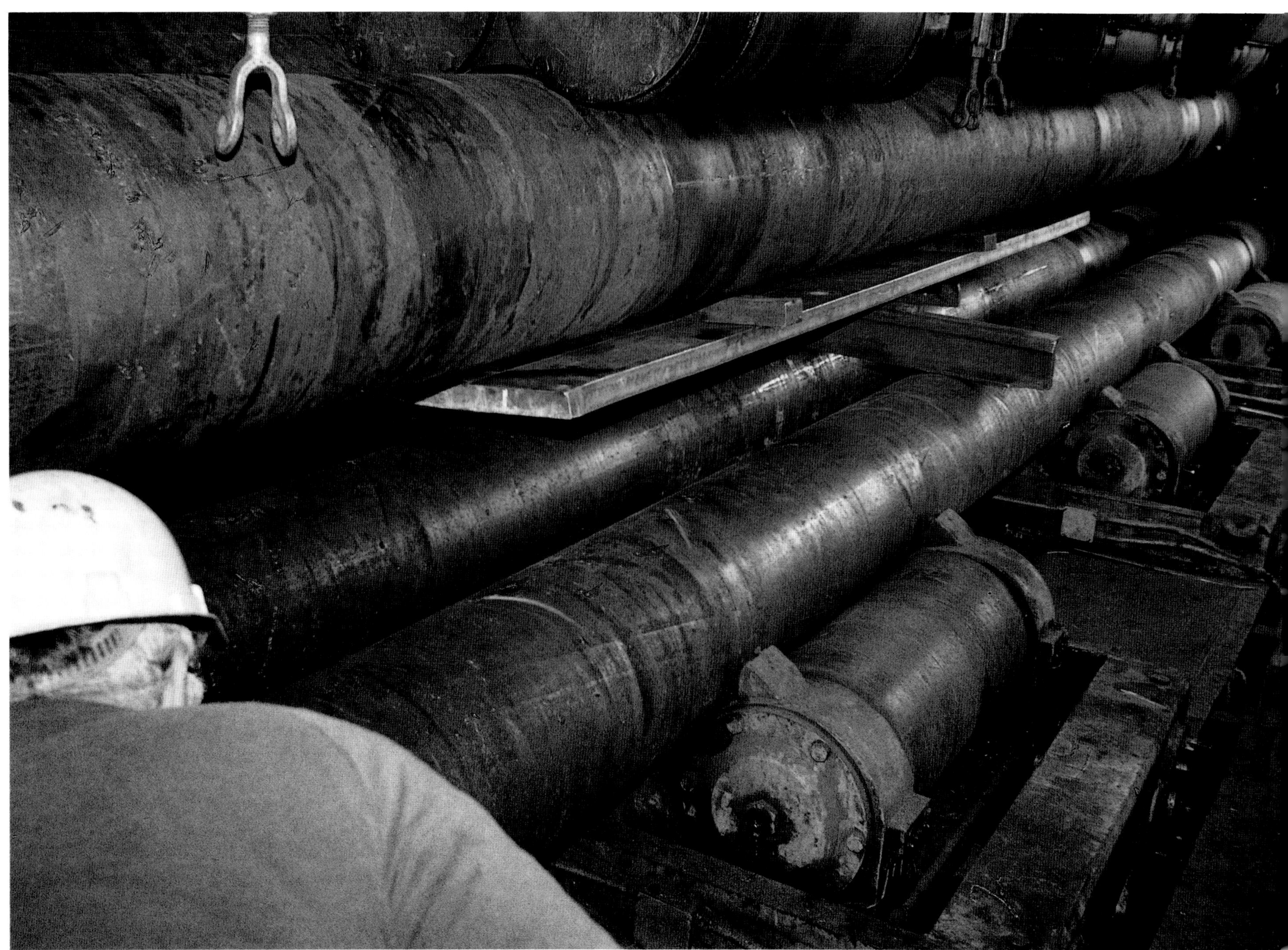

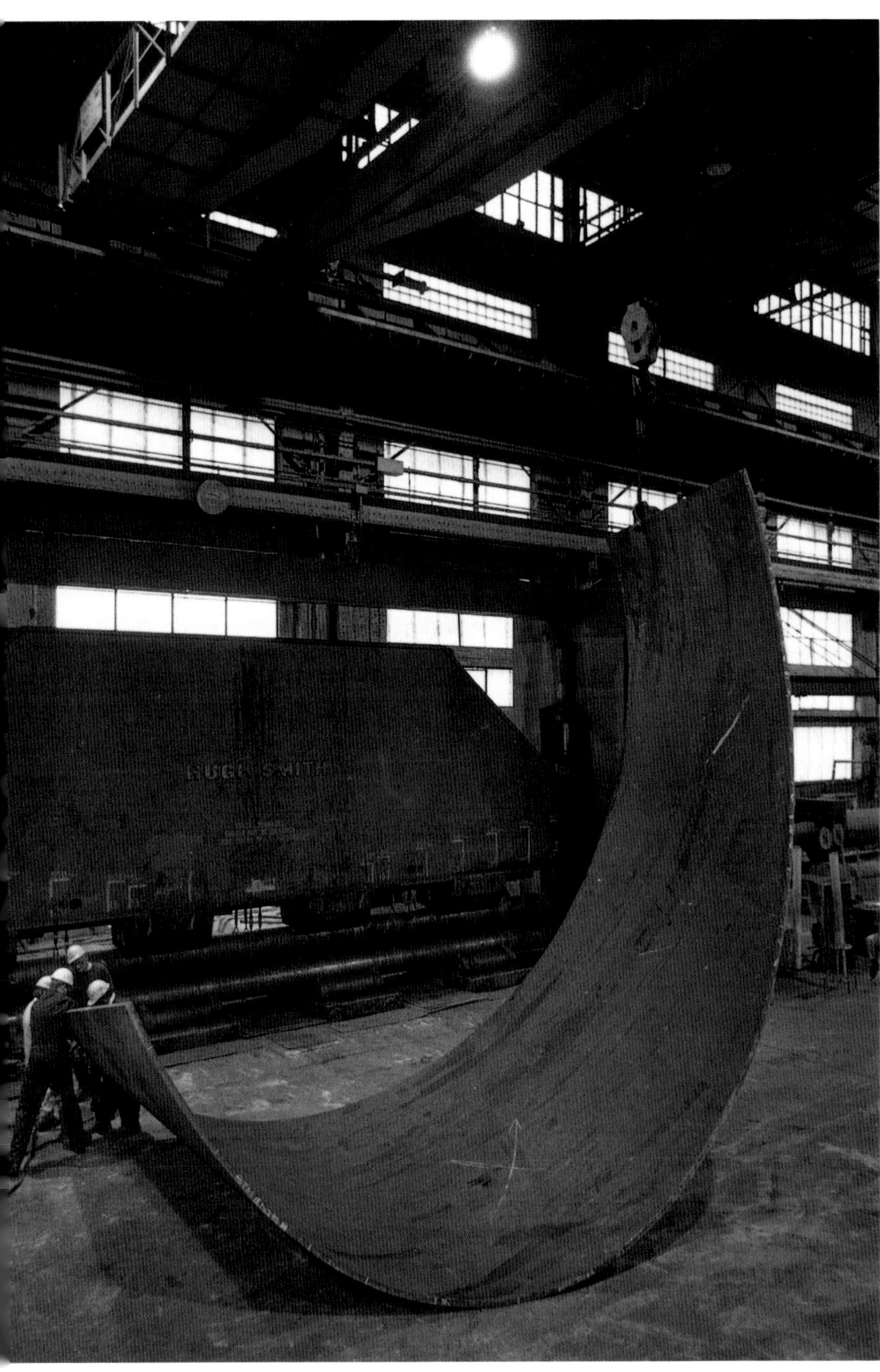

inside or outside, is that because the surface is continuously inclined, you don't sense the distance to any single part of the surface. It's very difficult to know exactly what is going on with the movement of the surface.

Once we started to use the wheel as a torquing device to generate the models, we realized that we were on to something. Subsequently, we've made over thirty models, although we've only built four full-scale sculptures. There's a big range left. After four, you can see where the potential is, what's excessive, what needs to be enlarged upon, and what to avoid.

LC: Richard, given that you're shaping a void, does that mean these works will all be autonomous, that they will never become site-specific?

RS: Well, they're not site-specific, but I don't think they're autonomous either. *Olson* and *Intersection* weren't site-specific pieces. None of the conical pieces I've made was site-specific. *Tilted Arc* was a different case in that it's a cylinder tilted into the ground, in a specific place, in relationship to a specific context, commissioned for that context.

In terms of ideal conditions for siting the Torqued Ellipses, I am interested in an external architectural referent; the outside of the form reads better, its definition is clearer, in relation to a vertical plane than it would be in relation to a flat open landscape. I'm very happy with them in the space they're in now. You immediately see the five-foot overhang of *Torqued Ellipse I* because of the wall next to it.

These pieces break with the tradition of autonomous sculpture in that there's no gestalt reading. You don't know the form even if you walk around it several times. When you walk inside the piece, you become caught up in the movement of the surface and your movement in relation to its movement.

As to the movement of the plane, the only precedents I can think of have occurred in figurative sculpture, on the exterior of the form as, say, an elbow turns, or a knee bends, or a back humps. The only comparison I can think of as far as the experience of interior space is concerned would be walking inside the Buddha of Kamakura or the arm of the Statue of Liberty; in those cases you're actually inside the volume as it's rotating. There is no other situation I know of in sculpture where that condition occurs—nor in architecture, because most architects who use tilted curves build conical sections. I don't know of anyone who has used a torqued ellipse.

LC: How did you know that a twelve-foot plate would not be adequate for these works?

RS: If you start with a twelve-foot rectilinear plate and cut the S-curved template out of it, the width of the plate, that is, the height of the final sculpture, will be considerably less. If you start with a sixteen-foot plate, you can probably get a thirteen-foot-high piece. If you start with a twelve-foot plate, you will only get a nine-foot-high sculpture. If they're leaning five feet out and five feet in, these nine-foot pieces aren't going to have the same capacity to cohere, hold, or envelop the space as a twelve- or thirteen-foot-high piece: the higher the elevation, the greater the potential for the torquing to have an effect.

In this group at Dia, the first piece is twelve feet high, and the others, *Torqued Ellipse II* and *Double Torqued Ellipse*, are thirteen feet. Even one additional foot in elevation gives the piece more of a vertical lift. There's no way of making them higher than thirteen or fourteen feet because the limit of any roller in the world is sixteen feet and plates are not made wider than sixteen feet. When I thought I was not going to be able to make these pieces in steel, several architects advised me to build them in concrete. But the problem with making them in concrete—where you can go as high as you want—would have been that they would be compared to architecture. I wanted to keep them within the definition of sculpture, I did not want to start begging issues that seem irrelevant to sculpture. If they were any larger and of concrete, they could be compared to the contained spaces of architecture. Also, built in concrete, these pieces would totally lose the tension of the torqued steel, which affects your experience of their space. There is a stress put on the steel that you register.

LC: If you build in concrete, you're not working with a given element.

RS: That's right. You're constructing, you're making a form, where you necessarily have to use a Rebar skeleton. The pragmatic efficiency of concrete is more within the tradition of Russian Constructivism.

LC: Is the thickness of the plate determined by engineering considerations?

RS: It could be thinner. I've decided on two inches because I want stability in the form. You only see the

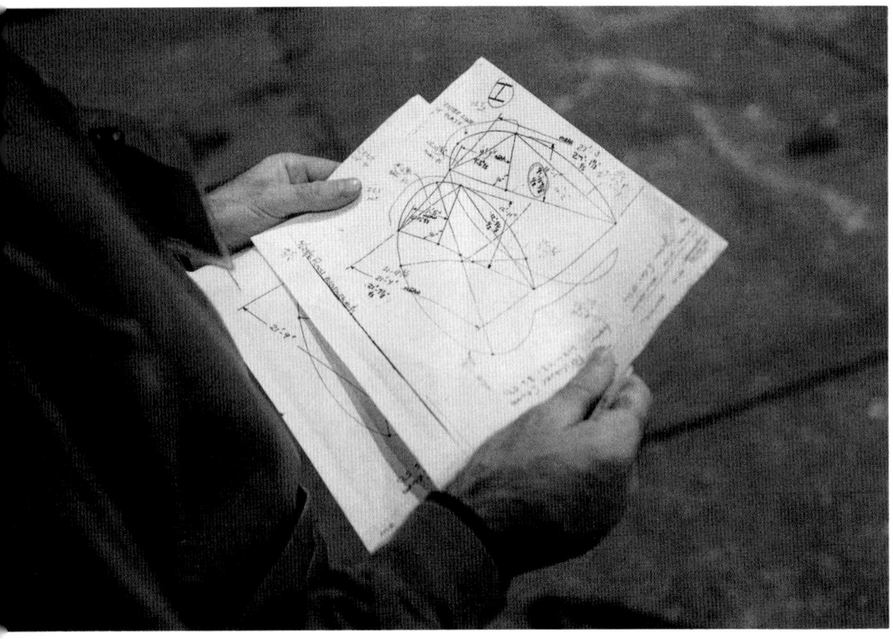

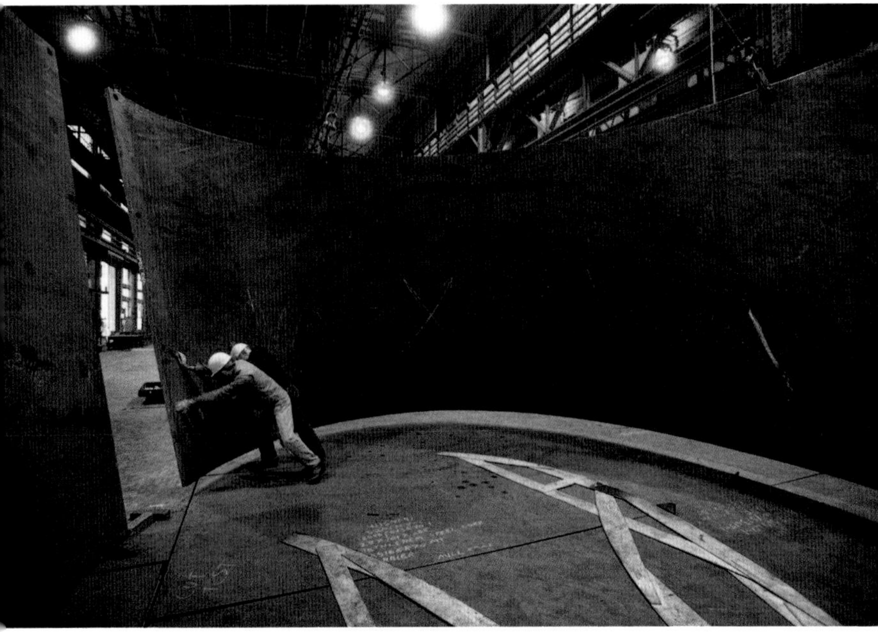

thickness at the edges of the opening where you enter, since you can't see either the top or the bottom. The cut is the only indication of the weight of the plate. We probably could take them down to an inch and a half, but then the form would start to get flimsy. Each plate weighs twenty tons, each sculpture forty tons, yet they don't seem heavy. Because of their movement, there's a certain weightlessness to them. You don't sense their heaviness or the gravitational load. They seem to spin.

LC: Given that you have developed almost thirty models, how did you choose which ones to realize first?

RS: We wanted to begin with the one that was the most extreme: that's the one where the ellipses are at right angles to each other. Then we made *Torqued Ellipse III*, which isn't in the exhibition at Dia. It's almost cylindrical, the overhang is very subtle, only about a foot and a half in either direction. The one with a fifty-five-degree angle is a more elongated ellipse. From looking at the models, we decided that within the range, the fifty-five degree was at the far extreme to the ninety degree. Then, in order to build the ellipse inside the ellipse, we had to find two that would allow us to deal with the relationship of the inside of one to the outside of the other; where the lean would maintain a certain circularity of the form. We found that a seventy-degree angle would work better than a ninety degree, because with a ninety degree, where the overhang approaches five feet, the outer would be too far away from the inner ellipse.

One of the key features of these sculptures is that their outside is totally different from their inside. From the outside, you have no sense of what the form is on the inside; and when you're in the inside, it is very difficult to understand how the form leans on the outside. They challenge your memory. They are unlike any space you know. Since you don't have any threshold experience to go back to, you are relegated to your experience in the space, and unless you have been around them a long time, they're very difficult to figure out. They require more than one or two viewings.

I don't think that knowing the angles at which the top and bottom ellipse relate to each other has to do with the content of the work; that's just something that informs the work.

LC: Why did you decide to place those particular three together in the gallery? Can you say something about the decisions involved in choosing to align them?

RS: At first I thought it might be best to show one at a time. But that seemed a little presumptuous, if not impossible, given the costs of each single installation. Also, I wasn't interested in putting the accent on their uniqueness. I was more interested in pointing out how one develops out of the other, how one differs from the other. Two sculptures would have been read as isolated spaces, they would not have entered into a relationship with each other. In order to understand the differences, there needed to be three in a triangulated space.

If you play one off another, the sculptures themselves teach you how to read them. The first two reveal themselves more explicitly. The experience of the third, *Double Torqued Ellipse*, is more protracted. You enter into a concentric elliptical space. There are radical differences between *Torqued Ellipse I* and the double ellipse in the ways in which anticipation and memory come into play, the containment of the space, and the entry into their interiors.

There are some occasions when a single piece is totally satisfactory in that it brings the problem of an entire series to a didactic conclusion so that there is no need to build any more. This doesn't seem to be the case here, where each work seems to be complex enough in its variation and its modulation to be satisfying in and of itself. I'm not worried about making the definitive piece in this group, I'm more concerned with making a body of work, which allows me to see how the language plays out.

LC: Has there been another occasion when you've had such a systematic, or such a continuous play with a set of problems?

RS: With the Props. First they were against the wall, then in the open space, then there were weights overhead, holding plates up underneath. The whole propping problem produced a body of work that I thought was fairly open-ended.

I have never before worked on a series where I was so convinced about the necessity of continuing, even though initially I had a lot of doubts about where it was going, what it was going to be, and even whether it was ever going to be done. As I said before, it has taken over three years just to get these four pieces built. This has been a long haul for me. I haven't stayed with many problems for this long.

LC: Are there related drawings?

RS: Drawings were made from the models using the CATIA computer program. I didn't begin by making sketches. I never work from drawings.

LC: Are they sometimes formed in parallel, simultaneously?

RS: There are some artists who have an image in mind, then make a drawing, and then a sculpture. I work completely opposite to that. I make a model, make the sculpture, and then I might make drawings. But these drawings never explicitly describe the sculpture, or point to the sculpture. I deal with drawing as an autonomous activity, as a different area of work, one that has to do with the materials that are invested in making the drawing. So far, there are no drawings coming out of these sculptures.

LC: Do you have a sense there could be?

RS: I don't think so. But, things have a way of cross-breeding, and there are causalities and references that I don't foresee. At the moment, I doubt it.

Michael Govan: The one variable you've left untouched is the ground plane in this series.

RS: At Dia, you don't sense the architecture: what you sense is the concrete, the steel plates, and the wooden trusses overhead, their interlacing and cross-bracing. The building is reduced to the floor, the ceiling, and the skin of the steel volumes. The content between floor and ceiling becomes integrated into the pieces. If you took these pieces outside or if there was a higher space or a clearer definition of the ceiling, you would be able to read the ellipse at the top more easily as a regular shape rotated in relation to the bottom ellipse. Here at Dia, the trusses interfere with reading the edge of the top ellipse.

All those conditions come into play when reading the pieces. The concrete and the wood overhead encapsulate the volume. The walls seem to disappear. You don't sense them, just as you don't sense the length of the space. When you walk into the room, you're not in a room with pieces in it, you're in the space of the pieces.

LC: Was this solution the only possible configuration?

RS: I didn't want to show *Torqued Ellipse III* given that, compared with the other two, its scale didn't seem to hold up. I think it would have stood apart. These pieces definitely share a contained language, and I wanted to keep them together.

LC: I'm interested, too, in the fact that the viewer, the participant, seems to need to be in constant motion, perhaps more so than in any of your other works. In many of those that involve curves, there is still a primary view, or there is a viewpoint where things cohere. However, there seems to be no ideal viewpoint in these. There's no one moment when you have an overall or synoptic understanding.

RS: When you walk into the center of these Ellipses, without thinking about it, you keep turning your body in order to understand their space. Even when you're standing still in the center, it's destabilizing because you don't quite know how the steel is torquing, toward you or away from you. The disorientation you might feel, or the "destabilization" of the space, seems to be part and parcel of your movement. This feeling has to do with the fact that your coordinates are challenged in terms of where things are in relation to your body, and how they are moving, or where you've been in relation to a space in front of you, or behind you. Your

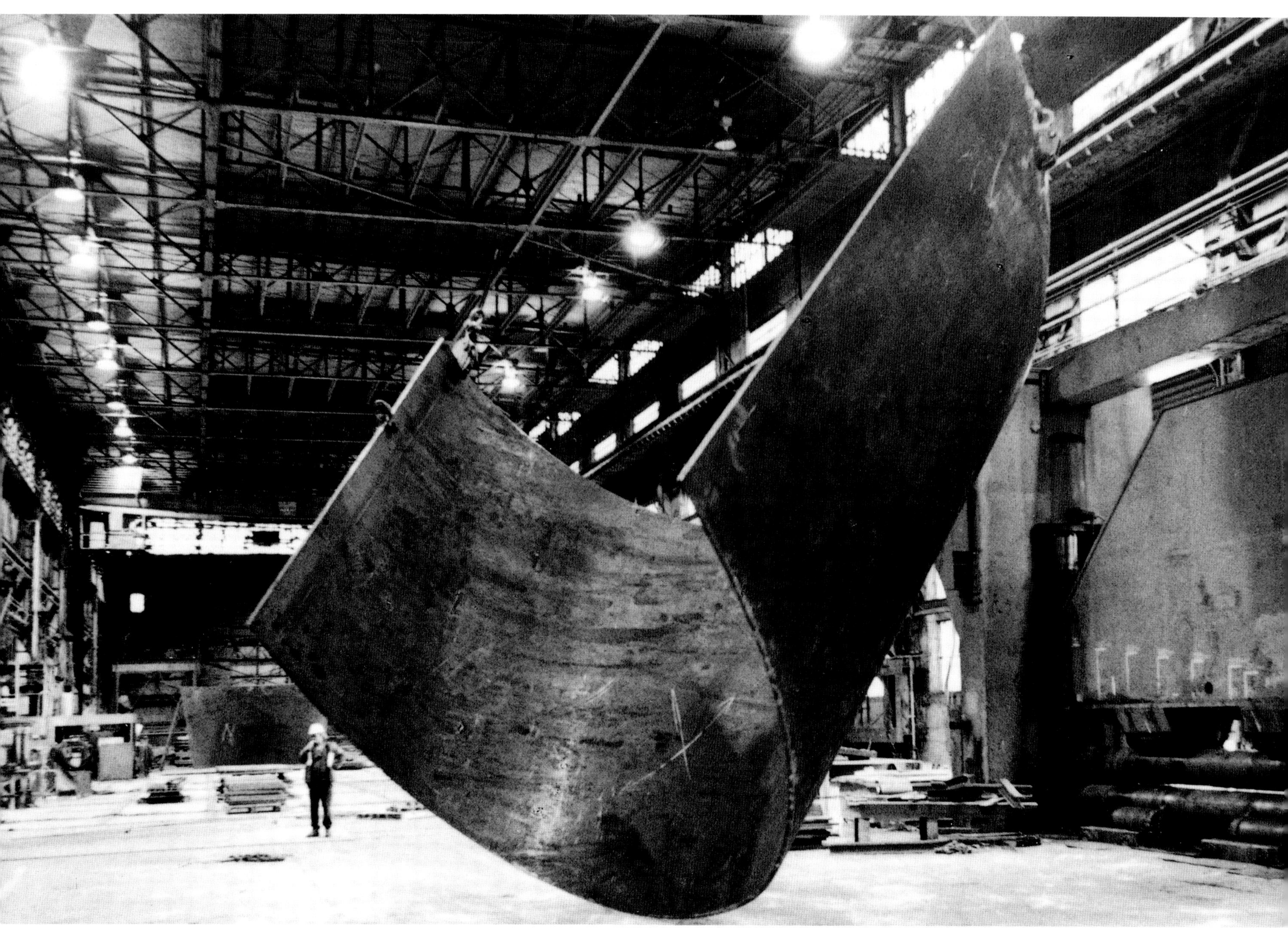

orientation to what's above and below and right and left is called into question. It's hard to keep track of where you think you are going because the curvature of the volume is constantly changing. You become implicated in the tremendous centrifugal force in the pieces. In relation to the space of the entire exhibition, there is a decentering.

MG: There's an irony in the fact that they are so decentering and destabilizing, and yet there's an absolute rigor and logic to their structure. The weight is balanced—

RS: There's no tendency for them to overturn. They're totally stable. And they're rigorously put together. They're butted up, there's no internal joint. They are exact down to the millimeter.

LC: One comparison I first thought of was with a Tiepolo ceiling painting. Depending upon where you enter the room and how you move, the whole composition, its focus and balance, and even the pose of any individual figure seems to alter. You mentioned Guarini.

RS: Or Borromini. If you enter Borromini's San Carlo from a side aisle, you read the space as an illusion. As soon as you walk to the center, it turns out to be totally coherent. The space rises straight up and doesn't change in its regular oval form from top to bottom. It is kind of an "oval cylinder." For me, walking in from the side aisle was more interesting than standing in the central space. Then it occurred to me that I could possibly take what I perceived from the side aisle, and torque the space.

MG: These works are very rigorous and logical in terms of process and procedure, and yet there are effects of illusion. Is that a by-product, an after-effect?

RS: When I think of illusion, I always think of something purporting to be something other than what it is, or I think of Mannerism, where there's heightening of the form for effect. I've never been particularly interested in illusion, nor do I think that these works are illusionistic. I can understand when you say that if you lose your sense of where the plane is, then you may feel that you're in a space that has an illusionistic dimension to it, but these pieces are not illusionistic in a sense that they purport to be something other than what they are.

MG: There's also the whole issue of the relativity of space-time. These works seem to make you feel the relativity of space.

RS: That's what's strange about this work—and I have no way of explaining it—the volume of the space you're in seems to be physically moving. You can say it's just the result of the skin moving in and out, but you actually sense the space as moving. Now, that may be illusionistic, but it's not something that I could have anticipated. It's not that I'm not interested in it, I just don't even know how to program such a space. I'm definitely interested in it once it has occurred. I still feel vulnerable about these works, because I'm not sure of their readings.

MG: While obviously inherently stable and non-malleable in one sense, steel seems here to have been pushed to an edge of what it can do.

RS: I'm using steel now almost like you would use rubber, in a very elastic way. That's something that hasn't come up in my work since a very early piece,

To Lift (1967), where I took a piece of rubber, lifted it up, and the form it attained was a result of the gravitational pull. We made lead models of the elliptical pieces, because lead is malleable, and once we could make small-scale lead models with the wheel, we figured it might be possible with a dense enough roller with great compression to make them in steel. If there was another material that I thought would give me the same compression and torquing of space, I would have no reason not to use it. I just don't know what it would be. Also, I happen to know more about steel than about other materials.

The selection of material ends up being very personal and private. I don't want to be at the receiving end of the standardized use of material. I would like to be able to use material to invent forms that haven't been invented before. And I'd like to try to make something that I don't know anything about, that is a new condition to me. If you can take your material, whatever it is, and apply it to that need, then possibly you can make the material do something it hasn't done before. In terms of forming, these pieces probably look more plastic than anything you have ever seen in steel.

You have to grow with a material and understand its potential if you're going to work your way through what it can offer in its own language. I've been around steel all my life.

MG: Do you think you've sensed the edge of the potential for steel?

RS: Hardly. I'm just starting. I think these pieces open the problem for me.

LC: Is there anything available now, such as computer technology, that makes these works possible in a way that was not the case, say, thirty years ago?

RS: The computer allows us to lay out the radial lines on the template for the roller to follow in bending the plates. We could have made traditional engineering drawings. That would have served the same purpose. It just would have taken longer. And, in addition to simplifying and speeding up the design process, the CATIA program can simulate a three-dimensional cage volume, which is helpful.

Someone asked me what a cross-section would be halfway up *Torqued Ellipse I*—where the ellipses are torqued at right angles to each other. To me it makes no difference whether it's not something you experience. Your experience of these works doesn't reduce them to their logic. And even if you do understand the logic, it may not be the content.

LC: They differ radically from Minimalist work, from,

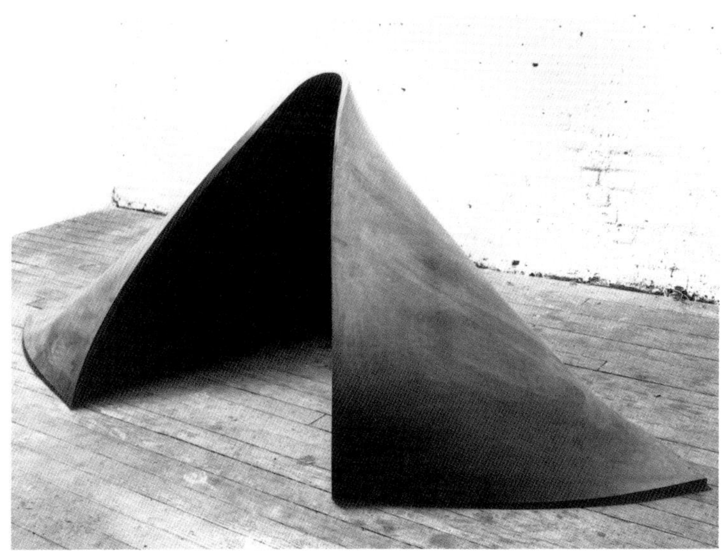

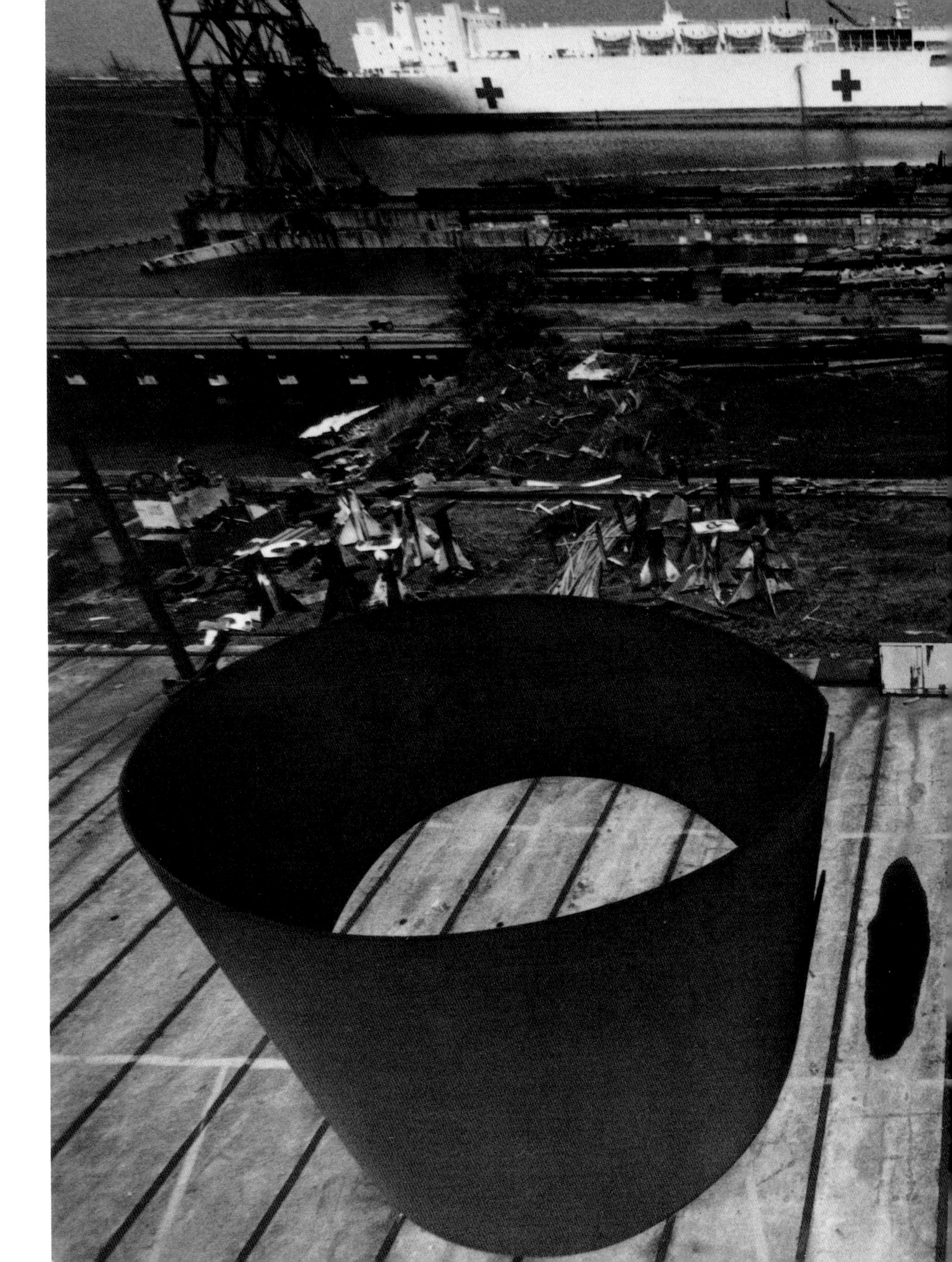

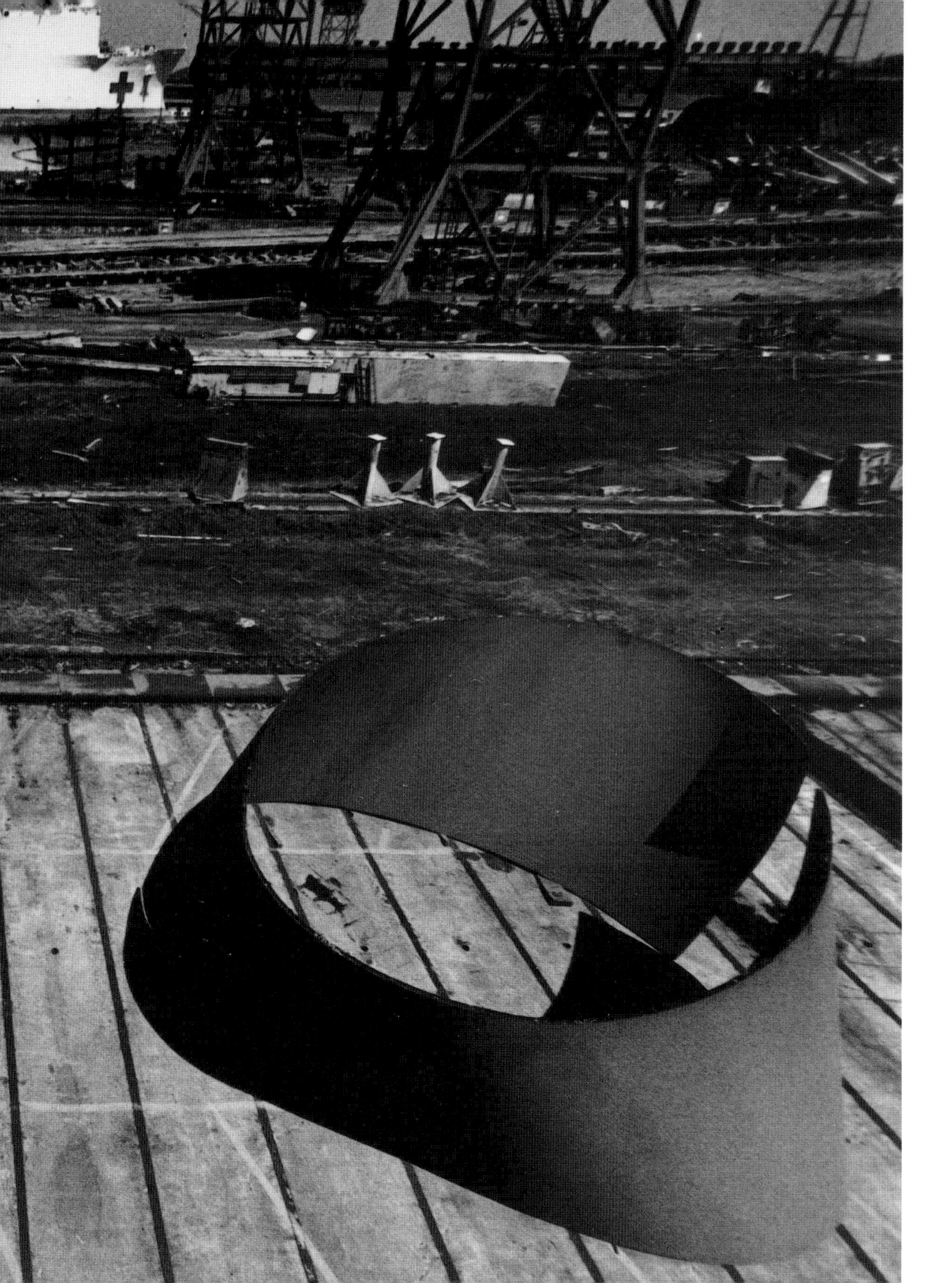

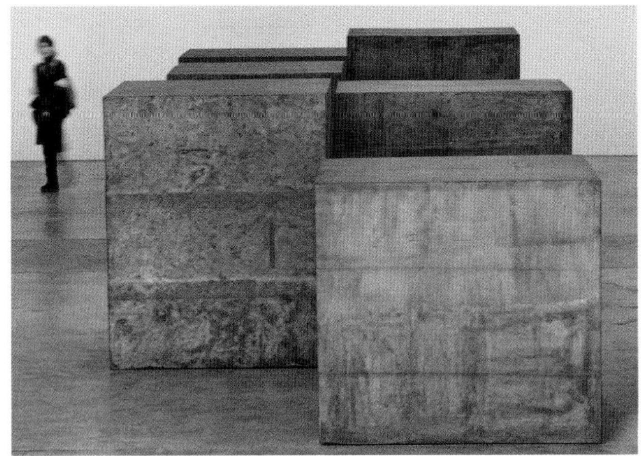

say, a Donald Judd box, whose ideal form one immediately understands very clearly, and yet one's experience of it always remains a matter of contingent perceptions in relation to a perfect form, a singular image.

RS: Space here has become a material for me. I'm trying to deal with the substance of space, to make it affect your body in ways that haven't happened before. These pieces aren't primarily predicated on your eye, as much as on the movement of your body. They're the least optical pieces I've ever made. They have very little to do with seeing something as a thing, as an object. Basically you're walking and relating to an experience of space that you could not have doped out with your eye.

I think Judd's a great sculptor, but when he emerged, he had a real desire, or need, to get away from the history of sculpture up to that point. He and Dan Flavin both wanted to make works that were neither sculpture nor painting. They state as much in their writing. They gravitated toward an extension of painting, not an extension of what sculpture had been up to that point. I came to sculpture with a different set of assumptions. I came to sculpture in relation to its space, its mass, its material, its gravity, and its possibilities in structuring an open field.

In a piece such as *58 x 64 x 70* (1996), space evaporates when you walk up close to the blocks. Because of the enormous amount of weight of the forged steel, you're aware of the density of the load, you don't even sense the space. It's as if it has been obliterated by the fact that there's this enormous mass in front of you. These pieces here are another way of pointing to the substance of space as material, which is very different from the approach to sculpture that came out of an extended painting concern and that sought a counterpart to a three-dimensional space with a precedent in painting.

LC: In a plane?

RS: Yes, in a plane. One of the things that probably will interest architects in these pieces is that they are generated by line. Architects usually generate structures with planes. They think about planes in relation to planes, not about the lines that generate the planes. And when you get into the analysis of computer programs and numbers, that takes you even further away from the plane, or from any literal element that generates space. I guess that's why Rick Smith thought when I told him what I was doing that finding the solution to the problem by using the wheel was endearing; it's not the way engineers or architects think when they're programming numbers.

What interested Frank Gehry's office in the Ellipse

project was that it represented the total opposite of the construction of the Guggenheim Museum in Bilbao, which is built like a traditional nineteenth-century sculpture, where the skin is wrapped around the inside and outside of an armature. The steel Ellipses establish the entire form, the inside and the outside, with one material. Frank's staff could immediately see their potential for building. So I've been able to work with his office very easily. For me, it's an invaluable open situation which greatly facilitated the process of getting these pieces underway.

LC: Does it have more than practical consequences or advantages? Is watching architecture being generated a way of also differentiating, of making very clear to yourself, the boundaries between sculpture and architecture?

RS: Most of my reading is in architecture, and most of what I use for comparisons in terms of my work is related to architecture. I share a common language with architects in that I work with the same generic spaces, the same scale. Nonetheless, my work is core-driven by sculpture, and the potential for sculpture.

Right now, I find writing on architecture more interesting than the writing on contemporary sculpture because most of the writing on sculpture always harks back to painting. It's very strange, but nobody writes about the condition of sculpture: they write about the condition of painting and then talk about sculpture. Sculpture is defined as any- and everything that is not painting. When I read Peter Eisenman, Rem Koolhaas, Tadao Ando, Daniel Libeskind, or others whose work I follow quite closely, I come away with other ways of thinking about the potential for sculpture—most often in contradiction to their position. Critical theory and most writing in the art field is less interesting to me.

MG: Do you read about physics or issues related to space?

RS: I've read a lot by Freeman Dyson, a physicist who makes the fantasy of physics applicable to one's imagination. We have a conversation going. He's the only physicist I read.

LC: And did you read writers such as Bachelard?

RS: Sure, although most French theory hasn't been very useful to me. I am more interested in a writer like Blanchot. But after a point, you have your own problems, your work comes out of your own work.

MG: When talking about the early seventies you said that in relation to movement in space you found most interesting ideas that were explored in dance rather than in sculpture. Do you continue to be fascinated by dance?

RS: I don't follow dance the way I did in the sixties. When I first came to New York, the people who were the most generative in turning over ideas about body and movement, the potential of material in relation to organizing space, and behavior in relation to structure were dancers. They happened to be mostly women: Yvonne Rainer, Tricia Brown, Lucinda Childs, Deborah Hay, Simone Forti. Later on there was the Grand Union. There were probably others whom I'm overlooking. They provided the stimulus. For me, their performances opened up ways of relating movement to material and space, allowing me to think about sculpture in an open

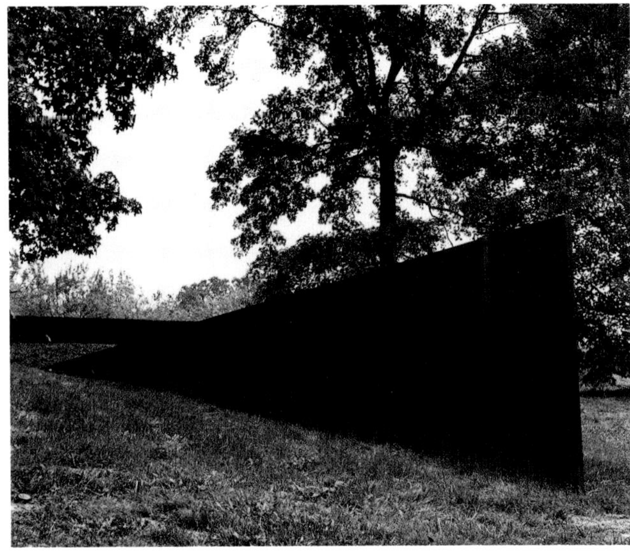

and extended field in a way that is precluded when dealing with sculpture as an autonomous object. I probably learned more from watching women perform in the early sixties, particularly Yvonne Rainer, than I did from looking at Minimalist art.

MG: Does that stay with you?

RS: It does. *Rose Fractions* (1969), for example, was a big piece for me. It sounds so trite, yet I found very important the idea of the body passing through space, and the body's movement not being predicated totally on image or sight or optical awareness, but on physical awareness in relation to space, place, time, movement. Those things were pushed to the fore by the dancers, and I picked up on them. It moved the situation from a pictorial concern, or an image concern, to a spatial concern. My early development had to do with placing pieces in relation to the space and the context, and with what happened with the space in between, rather than dealing with some contained notion of an object within space.

LC. Was that reinforced by seeing and walking through gardens in Japan?

RS: I think that happened simultaneously. I went to Japan in 1970 right after watching those performers in New York. Previously, in 1965 and 1966, I had lived in Florence, where the Renaissance idea that measured space in orthogonals prevailed. The Zen gardens were the antithesis to that, in that your vision is peripatetic and not reduced to framing an image. It includes and is dependent upon memory and anticipation. In terms of the potential of sculpture, I probably learned more in six weeks in Kyoto than I did in a year in Florence.

Once sculpture got off the pedestal and away from the figure, a whole host of other issues came up. Basically, they have to do with time and context. These concerns are somewhat divorced from the preoccupations of the Minimalists, who were more interested in the specificity of the object in its relation to the space. By contrast, I became very interested in the distribution of the elements in the open field, in the space in between. On returning to the U.S., I built *Pulitzer Piece: Stepped Elevation* (1970–71), which is comprised of three very large plates embedded in the ground over three or four acres. They act like barometers in the field, and function as surrogate horizons. You have to walk the entire field in order to see them. That piece was made directly in response to having lived in Kyoto.

Of course, there's a seepage factor. You don't really know how to apply what you're looking at when you're learning to see in a different way: sometimes it finds use later on. The relationship of time, space, walking, and looking—particularly in arcs and in circles—constitutes the only way you can see certain Japanese gardens. I spent a lot of time in them, a lot of time just thinking about what it was that I was looking at. The act of seeing, and the concentration of seeing, takes an effort. The gardens impose that effort on you if you want to see them. It's another way of ordering your vision, and it slows down your vision. That was helpful to me, very helpful.

MG: Many pieces, like Steve Oliver's *Snake Eyes and Boxcars* (1993), involve time and the dimension of moving, and, yet, these Torqued Ellipses are the first pieces where a contained space has an extended dimensional aspect.

RS: *Snake Eyes and Boxcars* takes at least an hour to see and the Pinault piece, *Elevations for L'Allée de la Mormaire* (1993), a good forty-five minutes. Like most of my work, these two pieces derive from my involvement with gravity, mass, weight, volume, placement, and orientation to space. In particular, they take all those considerations and push them in relation to the movement of your body in the open field of the landscape. There's no way that you can sum them up in a single image.

MG: The new works at Dia occupy only some six thousand square feet, yet there's an incredible amount of time packed into them.

RS: I've always been interested in trying to make something that has no equivalent in terms of nature or anything that's been made. These pieces have no equivalent in terms of the spatial situations you've been in or you've seen before. That doesn't make them better or worse.

LC: They're time-based without being involved in illusionism...

RS: They're time-based, but they're not narrative. Since there's no hierarchy of views, there's no privileged position from which to understand them. But the only way to know them is through time. The time one needs for considering them is totally subjective, it is up to each individual viewer how he or she wants to deal with the space in relationship to his or her own awareness.

LC: With *Snake Eyes and Boxcars* and related works, as you go through them, you map a space. By moving from one point to another, you create a trajectory in the space, which somehow puts an imprint on it. But moving around these works at Dia, you are not putting an imprint on the ground because where your head is and where your feet are seem not to be aligned: what's going on at the level of your feet and what's going on at the level of your head are removed, quite distinct.

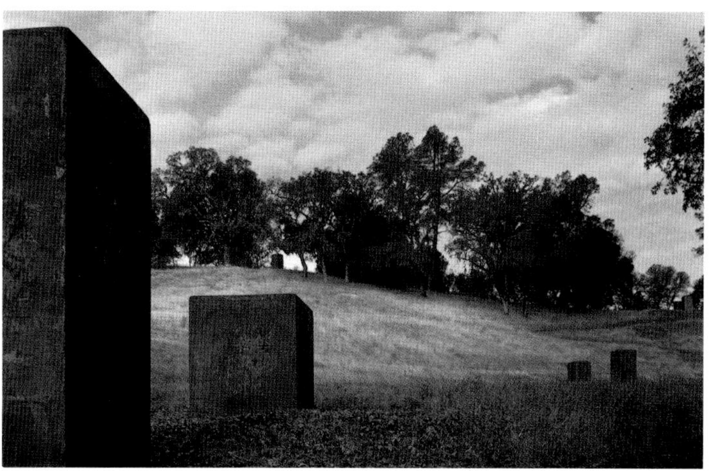

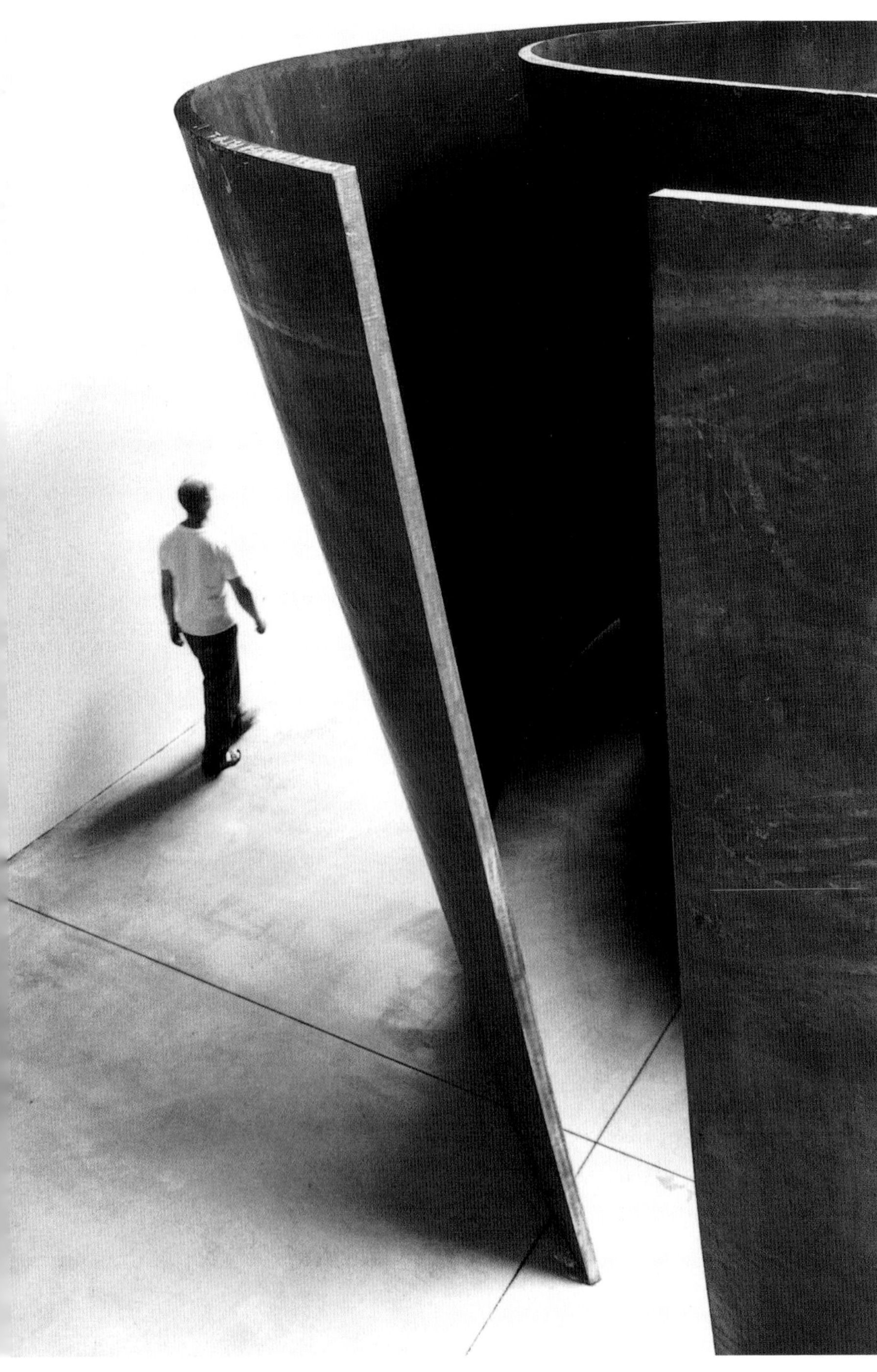

RS: That's right. In a piece like *Snake Eyes and Boxcars*, you're somewhat more directed in terms of the paths you take.

Here, what may happen is that your feet and your head are moving in two different directions at the same time; you may be turning your head in one direction while your feet are moving in the opposite way. That's one of the reasons for the disorientation you experience.

LC: As you walk in these, in *Double Torqued Ellipse* especially, your body responds to things your eyes are not yet even seeing. You have a bodily based reading which is not primarily a visual reading and, simultaneously, a visual reading.

RS: The first person who said that these pieces had nothing to do with looking was Peter Eisenman. He said they were generated totally by body movement. I hadn't distilled it down to such a limited idea of how they function, but in some sense it's true. You have to pay attention to where you're going, but—

LC: —your body is already—

RS: —reacting without even thinking about it. All one's movements are instinctual in order to navigate the space because you can't locate the distance of the plane that moves as you move. From one step to the next, you find that it's no longer moving away from you, it's moving toward you, and it's no longer behind you, it's over your head.

LC: You don't really know what you've seen. Your responses are faster than what you're cognizant of seeing.

MG: In some sense you don't know where you've been.

Turn your head and a wall could be anywhere.

RS: We sense volume before we can articulate it. That's not something esoteric, everybody does it. In a discussion like this, it's hard not to sound like you're resolving some phenomenological mystery. As soon as you start reducing it to how you see it, it takes away from the fact that your body and your haptic senses don't register in that way. Nor can such experiences be distilled into words. The words are always made up *behind* the experience, *after* the experience.

Cape Breton, July 10, 1997

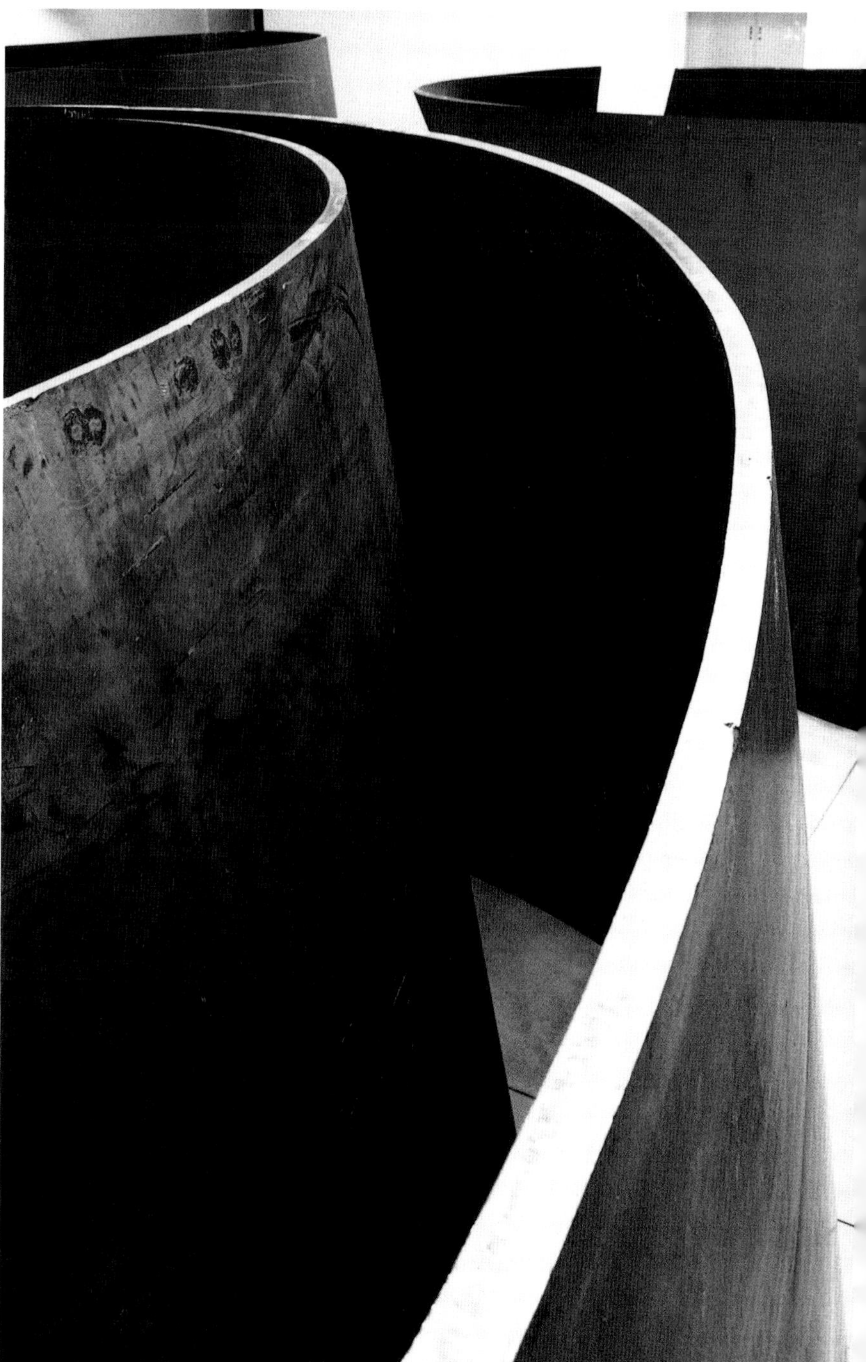

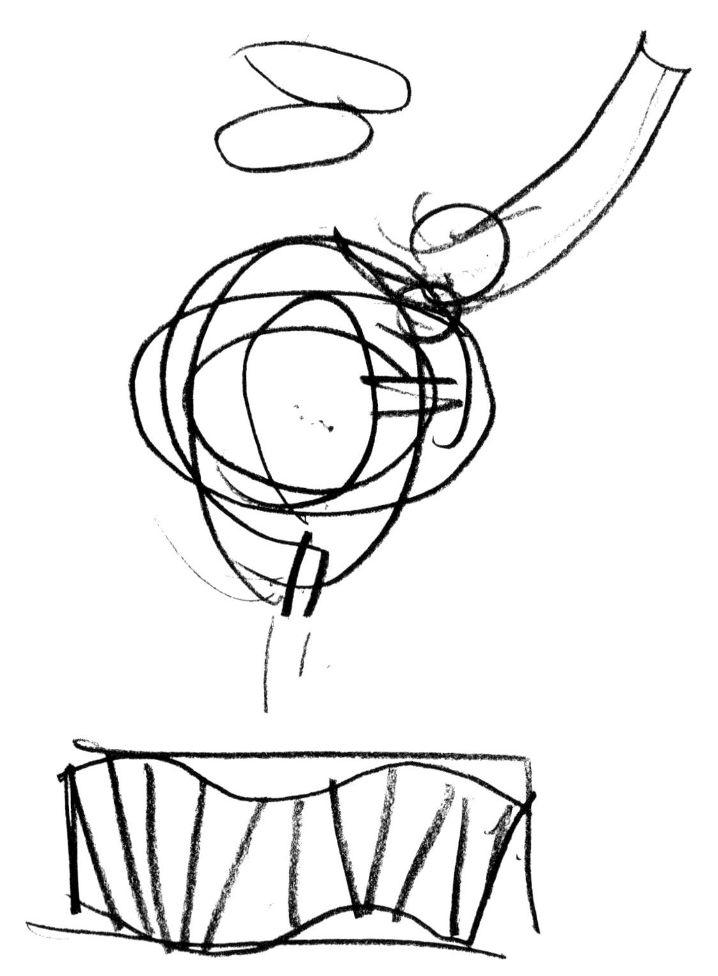
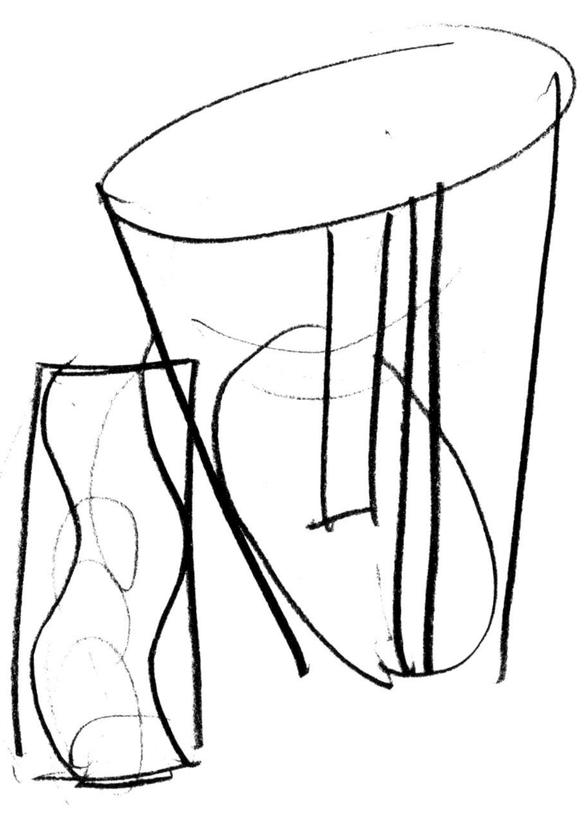

Learning Curves

Mark C. Taylor

to fold
to bend
to twist
to differ
to open
to knot

—Richard Serra

to space
to time

Richard Serra's art is difficult—difficult to make, difficult to display, difficult to comprehend, difficult to accept. This tends to provoke resistance: many regard his work as assertive, aggressive, even coercive. But this response oversimplifies the difficulty of his art. For Serra, art is difficult because it is complex. More precisely, art is *about* complexity. The difficulty of complexity and complexity of difficulty make the work of art demanding. When art is not simple, it not only takes time but, more importantly, gives time (its due).

Serra's exploration of the art of complexity began when his work took an unexpected turn. After studying literature at the University of California at Berkeley and Santa Barbara and painting at Yale, Serra spent a year in Paris and a year in Florence, where his interest gradually shifted from painting to sculpture. Then, in 1970, he lived for six weeks in Kyoto near the temple complexes at Myoshin-ji. During this first serious encounter with a non-Western culture, he spent many long hours reflecting on the Zen gardens associated with the temples. The experience transformed his understanding of art. As the artist recalled in a recent conversation: "My stay in Kyoto completely changed my ideas about sculpture."[1]

At first glance, this claim is puzzling, for nothing seems farther from the delicate refinement of Zen gardens than the raw power of Serra's signature works. But as one considers this unlikely association more carefully, surprising connections begin to emerge. Though drawing on different cultural and artistic traditions, Zen masters are preoccupied with many of the same issues as Serra. Their works present thoughtful meditations on the intricate interplay of emptiness/form, void/volume, lightness/weight, balance/imbalance, continuity/discontinuity, transience/permanence, and simplicity/complexity. In a 1992 interview with Lynne Cooke, Serra explains the significance of the gardens he discovered in Japan for the development of his work.

> The interior space of the temples is a dense, compressed volume, very simple and clear in terms of divisions and openings. I found the structure of the gardens more interesting than the temples. They are organized with a rigorous mode of placement. The primary characteristic of the garden is that the paths around and through them are curvilinear. The geometry of the site prompts walking in arcs. The articulation of discrete elements within the field and the sense of the field as a whole emerge only by constant walking and looking. Other gardens in Kyoto are laid out to be seen from a viewing porch. In some of them one element is hidden behind the other, and the entirety of the garden landscape is only revealed as one walks the length of the horizontal viewing platform of the temples. The layout of the gardens is based on the perceptual principles of time, meditation, and motion. This concept of space is essentially different from our Western concept, which is based on central perspective and arranges all objects on a line emanating from the eye of a static viewer. In the Zen gardens, directions, continuity, and paths work together to deny a fixed measure.[2]

Different kinds of Zen gardens are created for different purposes, as this remark suggests.[3] Water gardens, dry gardens, and tea gardens vary in design as well as function. One of the distinctive differences in Japanese gardens is between those that are intended to be viewed from a distance, like a painting on a wall or a sculpture on a pedestal, and those that can be appreciated only by walking through them. Both types of garden can display either precise rectilinearity or evocative curvilinearity. Serra is fascinated by gardens that permit meditative wandering and is intrigued by the artistic possibilities of curvilinear shapes and forms:

> When I first started going to the gardens of Myoshin-ji, it became very apparent to me that you either walk horizontal to the view or you walk through the interior of the garden. Walking through the garden is predicated on time in relation to movement, which implies continual apperceptive experience based on anticipation and memory. This is very different from what I had discovered when I was a student in Italy looking at Donatello or in Paris looking at Giacometti. You cannot find a correlative to the gardens in the Western sculptural tradition.[4]

What Serra discovers in the gardens of Japan is a different sense of space. Unlike the perspectival space that has governed perception in the West since the Renaissance, space in the garden is inescapably temporal.

> The primary characteristic of both the temples and stone gardens was that the ambulatory paths around and through them were circular. The geometry of the sites prompted walking in arcs. The articulation of discrete elements within the field and the sense of the field as a whole emerged only by constant looking. The necessity of peripatetic perception is characteristic of Myoshin-ji. (p. 29)

"Peripatetic perception" is not merely visual but involves the entire body in all of its spatial and temporal complexity. When roaming through the garden, it becomes clear that there is no space without time and no time without space. The fabric of experience is constituted by the complex interweaving of space-time.

The Japanese have developed a specific term to designate this distinctive understanding of space-time, *MA*, which the architect Arata Isozaki explains in an essay entitled "Space-Time in Japan":

> While in the West the space-time concept gave rise to absolutely fixed images of a homogeneous and infinite continuum, as presented in Descartes, in Japan space and time were never fully separated but were conceived as correlative and omnipresent....Space could not be perceived independently of the element of time. Likewise, time was not abstracted as a regulated homogeneous flow, but rather was believed to exist only in relation to movements or spaces.... Thus, space was perceived as identical with the events or phenomena occurring in it; that is space was recognized only in its relation to time-flow.[5]

Rather than an *a priori* structure—be that structure objective (as in Newtonian physics) or subjective (as in Kantian philosophy)—space and time, as well as their experiential apprehension, are inseparable from bodily movement. Space-time, in other words, is a corporeal event, which is never fixed but always in transition. As the word *MA* suggests, the site of this transition is the interval.

> [MA,] "the natural distance between two or more things existing in a continuity" or "the space delineated by posts and screens (rooms)" or "the natural pause or interval between two or more phenomena occurring continuously," gives rise to both spatial and temporal formulations. Thus the word *MA* does not describe the West's recognition of time and space as different serializations. Rather, in Japan, both time and space have been measured in terms of

intervals. Today's usage of the word MA extends to almost all aspects of Japanese life—for MA is recognized as their foundation. Therefore architecture, fine arts, music, and drama are all known as "the art of MA."[6]

As an event that occurs in an interval, which is never present as such, space-time is actually a spacing that is a timing and a timing that is a spacing. MA insinuates time into space by exposing the space of time. The art of MA—and there is no other art—is the art of spacing-timing.

A notion that approximates the spacing-timing expressed in the word *MA* has unexpectedly emerged in recent years in Western critical discourse. Derridean deconstruction is, in effect, an extended meditation on the far-reaching implications of the eventualities of spacing-timing. In his influential essay, "Différence," Jacques Derrida stresses the intersection of space and time in the word *différer*, which is derived from the Latin verb *differre* and means both "to differ" and "to defer or delay." Attempting to capture the oscillating rhythms of *différer* by insisting that his neologism *différance* implies both temporization (*temporisation*) and spacing (*espacement*), Derrida writes:

> *Différer* in this sense is to temporize, to take recourse, consciously or unconsciously, in the temporal and temporizing meditation of a detour that suspends the accomplishment or fulfillment of "desire" or "will," and equally effects this suspension in a mode that annuls or tempers its own effect...[T]his temporization is also temporalization and spacing, the becoming-time of space and the becoming-space of time, the "originary constitution" of time and space, as metaphysics or transcendental phenomenology would say, to use the language that here is criticized and displaced.
>
> The other sense of différer is the more common and identifiable one: to be not identical, to be other, discernible, etc. When dealing with différen(ts)(ds), a word that can be written with a final ts or a final ds, as you will, whether it is a question of dissimilar otherness or of allergic and polemical otherness, an interval, a distance, spacing, must be produced between the elements, and be produced with a certain perseverance in repetition.[7]

Neither spatial nor temporal, spacing-timing is the condition of the possibility or, in Derrida's terms, the "originary constitution" of space and time. So understood, spacing-timing is the complex "site" of the emergence of everything that is present. This "originary constitution" is, however, a strange "origin" because it is never present as such. Nor, of course, is it simply absent. In a manner strictly analogous to MA, *différance* is the "interweaving" or "interlacing" that draws together presence and absence in the interval that defines their difference.

to sculpt

to draw

Richard Serra is obsessed with drawing. He is rarely without a notebook in which he draws and redraws incessantly. It is as if he thinks and speaks by drawing. The longer one ponders his drawing, the clearer it becomes that drawing is not only a means of expressing his ideas but is a mode of experience more "primordial" than thinking. Drawing is nothing less than the "origin" of ideas. "To draw a line," Serra insists, "is to have an idea. A drawn line is the basis of construction. To draw is to innovate in multiplicity. The line gives to the work an inexplicable definition. It defines and redefines structure. To cut is to draw a line, is to separate, to make a distinction" (p. 28). From this point of view, drawing obviously is not limited to the two dimensions of pencil and paper but can be a three-dimensional sculptural activity.

> I put down a ruler (or template) underneath five different materials, making a rectangle to the right and left of which I cut so that what was placed on top was divided into three parts. The line—a cut—was a way of making a division through diverse elements and separating the field. Cut as line reoccurs not only in all of the sculpture but later in the large black drawings. (pp. 54–55)

In this way, the act of drawing inscribes the spacing-timing that articulates the differences constitutive of every shape and form. Commenting on *Cutting Device: Base—Plate—Measure* (1969), Serra underscores the formative function of the cut: "the cut as line informs the material, the structure, and the process" (p. 28).

Serra's rapid dissatisfaction with these early works derives from his conviction that such "opticality" places needless limitations on the work of art: "I started building pieces very early (1968) that had to do with balance and weightlessness. Most of the pieces were closed. What disappointed me was that you couldn't enter into their physical space" (p. 47). What is missing from these early works is precisely the space that he had discovered in the Zen gardens of Kyoto. In order to create the space and time for experience that is more than visual, it is necessary to open the work of art in new ways.

The works grow larger and larger as the opening expands. No longer autonomous objects to be viewed from a distance, Serra's sculptures become open fields that draw one into their midst. In *Circuit I* (1972) and *Circuit II* (1972–86), he begins to create what he had described in Japanese stone gardens as "ambulatory paths." Four steel plates are situated in an empty room to form an

X, which is open at the center. The size of the plates (8' x 24' x 1" in the former and 10' x 20' x 2" in the latter) makes it impossible to view the work as a whole. Apprehending this work takes time; it is necessary to enter and walk around in it. The space of the work cannot be experienced apart from the time of movement. When roaming through these broken circuits, senses other than vision are engaged. Unlike the ambulatory paths of the Zen gardens, the course Serra charts in these works remains rectilinear. Moreover, the work is confined to the space of the gallery.

Though long interested in the complex interplay between work and site, Serra did not build anything in the landscape until shortly after his return from Kyoto. The Pulitzers, he recalls, "gave me the opportunity to work on an enormous piece of land—probably about four or five acres. This was just after I came back from Kyoto and the impression of the temples and stone gardens was still fresh in my mind. This experience had a big impact on me and resulted in an enormous shift in my work."[8] The extent of the influence of the Zen gardens on Serra during this period is evident in both *Pulitzer Piece: Stepped Elevation* (St. Louis, 1970–71) and *Shift* (King City, Ontario, 1970–72). Freed from the limitations imposed by gallery walls, the openness of the site

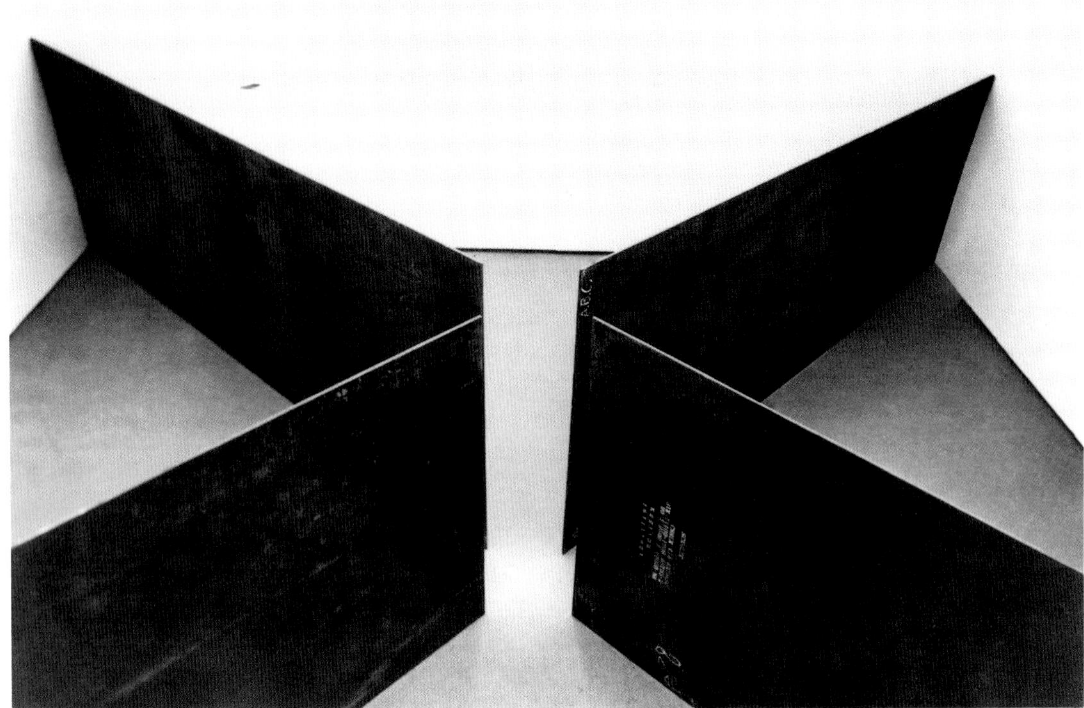

creates radically new possibilities for "peripatetic perception." Shortly after its completion, Serra described his purpose in *Shift*:

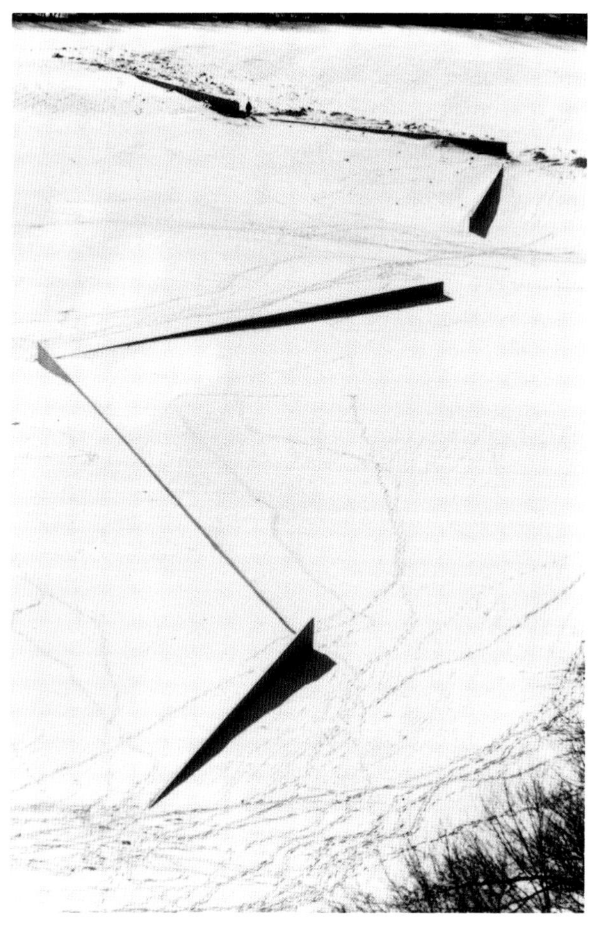

> The intent of the work is an awareness of physicality in time, space, and motion. Standing at the top of the eastern hill, one sees the first three elements in a Z-like linear configuration. The curvature of the land is only partially revealed from this point of view, because the configuration compresses the space.
>
> Until one walks into the space of the piece, one cannot see over the rise, as the hill descends into its second and third five-foot drop. This again is because the land's incline is inconsistent in its elevational fall....
>
> The work establishes a measure: one's relation to it and to the land...to [the land's] rise in relation to one's descending eye-level ....Insofar as the stepped elevations function as horizons cutting into and extending towards the real horizon, they suggest themselves as orthogonals within the terms of a perspective system of measurement. The machinery of Renaissance space depends on measurements remaining fixed and immutable. These steps relate to a continually shifting horizon, and as measurements, they are totally transitive: elevating, lowering, extending, foreshortening, contracting, compressing, and turning. The line as a visual element, per step, becomes a transitive verb. (p. 23)

As the work becomes transitive, it *shifts* from being a thing to being a process or from being a noun to being a verb. The "verbalization" of the work of art—which, for Serra, cannot be captured in language—presupposes the becoming-time of space and the becoming-space of time. The site of this transition is, as Serra suggests, the "cut" of sculpture. The opening and the work stand in a thoroughly paradoxical relationship: the cut opens the work, which opens the cut.

As the opening expands (and contracts), it grows more complex. On the one hand, the site becomes specific, while, on the other hand, the locus of the work becomes endlessly mobile. *Shift* is about this shifting/shifty site. Serra signals this shift when he notes, "The intent of the work is an awareness of physicality in time, space, and motion." Elsewhere, he elaborates this important point at length.

> From the top of the hill, looking back across the valley, images and thoughts are remembered which were initiated by the consciousness of having experienced them. This is the difference between abstract thought and thought in experience. The time of this experience is cumulative—slow in its evolution. One experiences a new kind of compression. The land is sensed as a volume rather than as a recessional plane, because from this point of view the valley has become abridged. For the first time, the alignment of the elevational steps is apparent. This alignment contracts the intervals of the space—not as drawing (or linear configuration) but as volume (as space contained).
>
> The space between the two sets of walls—across an open plane of approximately 120 feet—implies a center to the work. This center would coincide with both the measured center of the field and a gravitational or topological center of the land mass. However, this is not the center of the work. The work does not concern itself with centering in that way. The expanse of the work allows one to perceive and locate a multiplicity of centers.
>
> Similar elevations—elevations equal in height—in an open field, on a flat floor, shift both horizontally and vertically in relation to one's locomotion. Because of this, the center, or the question of centering, is dislocated from the physical center of the work and found in a moving center. (p. 13)

This is a critical text for any adequate understanding of Serra's contribution to the history of sculpture. His decentering of the work of art involves a thoroughgoing critique of linear perspective, which has informed art and determined perception since the Renaissance. An object that has no center is not an integrated whole but an open structure that never achieves closure. As the work is decentered, its site shifts, which is Serra's point when he stresses that "the expanse of the work allows one to perceive and locate a multiplicity of centers." These multiple centers, however, no longer are "in" the object; rather, "the center, or the question of centering, is dislocated from the physical center of the work and found in a moving center." The site of this moving center or these moving centers shifts from the object toward the subject. More precisely, the work of art becomes an event or process that occurs between the art object and the subject drawn (in)to it. As Rosalind Krauss shrewdly observes:

> By 1972 something fundamental had happened to Serra's conception of the cut. In that year he had made *Circuit* and *Twins*, in which cutting was no longer a force exerted on the patient body of the world outside the viewer, but was, somehow, what tied that world to the viewer, what shaped his perception, and, in so doing, could be shown to shape him. Intervening between the Base—Plate—Measure series and these later works, in 1969–71, was *Strike*, a sculpture conceived as performing a cut on space itself and organizing it in relation to the viewer's body, so that the interdependence of body and space—coming apart and being put back together—is choreographed in relation to the work.[9]

As the opening of the work of art becomes more complex, it implicates the subject by altering the very conditions of experience. This change is neither sudden nor momentary but takes time, which is given by the artwork. Serra puts time to work in the space of art. The timing of this spacing and spacing of this timing mark the difference between "abstract thought" and "thought in experience." Serra's sculpture creates the occasion for thought in experience, which transforms the experience of thought.

The argument staged in Serra's work extends beyond a criticism of classical sculpture to a critical engagement with the most basic tenets of modernist art and architecture. Responding to Peter Eisenman's inquiry about the significance of modernist sculpture's "break away from figuration or…representation in terms of figuration," Serra observes: "The biggest break in the history of sculpture in the twentieth century occurred when the pedestal was removed. The historical concept of placing sculpture on a pedestal established a separation of the object from the behavioral space of the viewer" (p. 141). The removal of the pedestal is necessary but not sufficient for overcoming the separation of object from the space of the viewer. The correlate of the autonomy of the artwork is the opticality of the experience of art. Insofar as modernist art remains committed to both the autonomy of the work of art and the principle of opticality, the gap between subject and object remains unbridgeable. Serra emphatically insists: "I'm not interested in looking at sculpture which is solely defined by its internal relationships" (p. 12). By rupturing the integrity of the sculptural work, he creates an opening for the reconfiguration of the subject-object relation and thereby recasts the experience of art. What distinguishes his sculpture from the work of artists such as Robert Irwin, Larry Bell, James Turrell, and Bruce Nauman is a shift away from a more or less exclusive preoccupation with opticality: "The way my work differs is that it's not opting for opticality as its content. It has more to do with a field force that's being generated, so that the space is discerned physically rather than optically" (p. 40).

Two closely related points in this telling comment deserve emphasis. First, if the work of art "has more to do with a field force that's being generated" than with a discrete, stable object, it can only be apprehended when what once was called "the viewer" is drawn into the play of forces constituting the work. Second, if the point of the work is not its opticality, perceptual experience must expand beyond the regime of the eye and its gaze to the entire body. Serra's mature sculpture, therefore, presupposes the primacy of bodily perception.

Serra's insistence that the work of art is not an integral object but a complex interplay between perceived object and perceiving subject is a direct response to the highly influential critique of Minimalism advanced by Michael Fried in "Art and Objecthood." Yve-Alain Bois has gone so far as to argue that "all of Serra's oeuvre is an implicit reply to Michael Fried's text."[10] Fried's argument is important in its own right as well as emblematic of the dominant version of modernism that Serra is intent on overthrowing. Responding to Robert Morris's claim that "the better new work takes relationships out of the work and makes them a function of space, light, and the viewer's field of vision," Fried charges Minimalism with a pernicious theatricality, which destroys the integrity and autonomy of the work of art by identifying the space of the work with the experience of the spectator.

> It may seem paradoxical to claim both that literalist sensibility [with which Fried associates Minimalism] aspires to an ideal of "something everyone can understand" (Smith) *and* that literalist art addresses itself to the beholder alone, but the paradox is only apparent. Someone has merely to enter the room in which a literalist work has been placed to *become* that beholder, that audience of one—almost as though the work in question has been *waiting for* him. And inasmuch as the literalist work *depends on* the beholder, it is *incomplete* without him, it *has* been waiting for him.[11]

In this remark, Fried indicates why he believes theatricality poses such a dangerous threat to art. The critical issue is *time*. If the work of art is not autonomous but depends on the "beholder" for its completion, it is always in a state of becoming and thus is irreducibly temporal. The purported autonomy and self-referentiality of the work represent efforts to negate time by securing the ideality and transcendence of the work of art. When the object is taken off its pedestal and opened to perceptive subjects without whom it cannot do its work, art is set in motion. Since the work of art is forever incomplete, the time of its becoming is endless.

> Endlessness, being able to go on and on, even having to go on and on, is central both to the concept of interest and to that of objecthood. In fact, it seems to be the experience that most

> deeply excites literalist sensibility, and that literalist artists seek to objectify in their work.... Here finally I want to emphasize something that may already be clear: the experience in question *persists in time*, and the presentiment of endlessness that, I have been claiming, is central to literalist art and theory is essentially a presentiment of endlessness, or indefinite, *duration*.[12]

Theatricality, in effect, secularizes the art object by knocking it off its pedestal and dragging it through the ever-changing world of quotidian experience. In his attack on theatricality, Fried struggles to resacralize art by immersing it in a moment that is an eternal present/presence.

> I want to claim that it is by virtue of their presentness and instantaneousness that modernist painting and sculpture defeat theater. In fact, I am tempted far beyond my knowledge to suggest that, faced with the need to defeat theater, it is above all to the condition of painting and sculpture—the condition, that is, of existing in, indeed of secreting, or constituting, a continuous and perpetual *present*—that the other contemporary modernist arts, most notably poetry and music, aspire.[13]

Though endless, Fried is convinced that this "perpetual present" is not haunted by the "endlessness" he sees in the "duration" of Minimalist art. Indeed, the "eternal now," he believes, overcomes the relentless temporality of ceaseless duration. When opticality is not "contaminated" by theatricality, the viewer is lifted out of time and enjoys a foretaste of eternity. Far from disappearing, religious aspirations repeatedly return under the guise of art. Fried translates this spiritual tendency in twentieth-century art into the language of criticism. But time relegates the vision of Fried and the artists he champions to the past. The present for which they long is never present but has always already passed away and thus can only approach as a future that never arrives. The space of this infinite delay is the tear of spacing-timing, which, for those who still believe in the transcendent ideality of art, inflicts a wound that never heals.

Sculpture's fall from its pedestal is the artistic equivalent of the death of the transcendent God. When the autonomy of the work of art is exposed as a sham, atemporal ideality gives way to temporal materiality. As the work of art enters time, time enters the work of art. Conversely, as time enters the work of art, the work of art enters time. No longer other-worldly, the "real" is incarnate in space-time. Incarnate art can only be apprehended carnally.

to body

to implicate

> The content of the drawing installations does not reside in the process of their making nor does it reside within the delineation of the field of a black canvas. The content resides in the viewer's experience of the space and place as it is redefined through the installation. For example, two black canvases on walls opposite each other compress and redefine the physical volume of the space and weight of the room. Your perception of the room is mediated through the drawing in terms of weight, space, place, and time. I am interested in the fact that when you are in a space that has been configured by a drawing, the sensation of time changes. (p. 255)

Space, time, and the body are bound in a knot that cannot be undone: space-time is unavoidably bodily and the body is inescapably spatial-temporal. This interpretation of the inherent corporeality of space and time and spatiality and temporality of the body represents a significant departure from the understanding of space and time that implicitly or explicitly informs most twentieth-century aesthetic theory and artistic practice. The decisive analysis of space and time for modern philosophy and art is presented in Kant's *Critique of Pure Reason*. Clement Greenberg argued that Kant's contribution to modernist practice is foundational: "I identify Modernism with the intensification, almost the exacerbation, of this self-critical tendency that began with the philosopher Kant. Because he was the first to criticize the means itself of criticism, I conceive of Kant as the first real Modernist."[14] Kant's influence on modernism is, however, considerably more subtle and complex than even Greenberg realizes. And nowhere is Kant's importance for art more evident than in his account of space and time.

Kant thoroughly transformed the interpretation of space and time advanced in classical philosophy, developed in Western metaphysics, and deployed in modern science. Space and time, he argues, are not characteristics of objects in the world but are the conditions of the possibility of subjective experience. The mind is not a *tabula rasa* as John Locke and his fellow empiricists believed, but has a definite structure that conditions all experience. At its most rudimentary level, the structure of the mind is constituted by the *forms* of intuition, which Kant identifies as space (external intuition) and time (internal intuition), and twelve categories of understanding. The forms of intuition and categories of understanding are *a priori*, i.e., they are prior to and independent of experience, and thus, Kant insists, they are universal. The mind, in other words, is hard-wired or preprogrammed. Knowledge involves a process in which the "raw" manifold of sensation is cooked first by the forms of intuition and then by the categories of understanding. Though the *content* of experience and knowledge varies, the *form* remains the same for all people in all places at all times.

Kant, in effect, translates the Platonic forms from the realm of ontology to the domain of epistemology. For Plato, the world is created through the agency of a demiurge, who brings together transcendent forms and mutable matter. In Kant's critical philosophy, the mind takes over this demiurgic activity. The world as we know it is created by the synthesis of the immutable forms of intuition and categories of understanding and the endlessly mutable manifold of sensation. In this way, the creative subject effectively displaces the creator God. Kant's appropriation of Plato's ontology for epistemological purposes leads to a paradoxical view of time as nontemporal and space as nonspatial. As *a priori* conditions of experience, time and space are unalterable and thus eternal. The immutability of space and time issues in the formal unity of experience for all rational subjects.

But what if the form and content of experience cannot be separated? What if *how* we experience is as mutable as *what* we experience? What if time is temporal and space is spatial? What if the primacy of perception transfigures the experience of thought? The English translation of Maurice Merleau-Ponty's *Phenomenology of Perception* appeared in 1962, and its impact on philosophy and art was immediate. The value of this analysis for artists was enhanced by his knowledge of, and interest in art. In *Phenomenology of Perception* as well as later studies like *The Visible and the Invisible* and *Sense and Non-Sense*, Merleau-Ponty draws on art to develop his argument and subjects particular artists and works to thoughtful analysis.

Serra was deeply impressed by Merleau-Ponty's insights. Though he studied *Phenomenology of Perception* while a student at Yale, it was not until he visited Japan that he really appreciated its importance for art.

> I read Merleau-Ponty while I was still at Yale but I did not really understand his work until I had been to Japan. I think that happens a lot of the time. You learn something but it's not useful to you. Even though some seepage occurs, there has to be a catalyst to make you rethink the information. That's what happened for me with Merleau-Ponty in Japan. And I knew it at the time.[15]

The bodily mediation of perception, which informs all conception, suggests new ways of understanding the constitutive role of sensation in artistic experience. Art—especially visual art—has always been associated with sensual experience. Indeed, the word *aesthetic* derives from the

Greek *aisthetikos*, which means "pertaining to sense perception." Yet, it is precisely this relationship between art and the senses that has for centuries rendered art suspect. From Plato to Hegel and beyond, critics have argued that the danger of art can only be overcome when reason controls the senses. Merleau-Ponty realizes that such control is impossible and admits that the struggle to achieve it inevitably leads to repression. Concluding his chapter entitled "Sense Experience," he argues:

> It is in the experience of the thing that the reflective ideal of positing thought shall have its basis. Hence reflection does not itself grasp its full significance unless it refers to the unreflective fund of experience which it presupposes, upon which it draws, and which constitutes for it a kind of original past, a past which has never been a present.[16]

This "original past…which has never been a present" is what subverts the possibility of the "continuous and perpetual *present*" for which Fried and many artists long. While this "original past" can be neither conceived nor comprehended, it can, Merleau-Ponty insists, be experienced. This experience is "pre-objective" and thus "pre-conscious." That which is pre-objective and pre-reflective is, however, also pre-subjective or, more precisely, is antecedent to the centered subject of consciousness and self-consciousness. Never crossing the threshold of consciousness, the "unreflective fund of experience" upon which reflection constantly draws derives from bodily perception.

> There is…another subject beneath me, for whom a world exists before I am here, and who marks out my place in it. This captive or natural spirit is my body, not that momentary body which is the instrument of my personal choices and which fastens upon this or that world, but the system of anonymous "functions," which draw every particular focus into a general project. Nor does this blind adherence to the world, this prejudice in favor of being, occur only at the beginning of my life. It endows every subsequent perception of space with its meaning, and it is resumed at every instant. Space and perception generally represent, at the core of the subject, the fact of his birth, the perpetual contribution of his bodily being, a communication with the world more ancient than thought.[17]

As this text suggests, Merleau-Ponty views the body as something like a topological knot that interlaces space and time. To understand his interpretation of perception, it is necessary to trace the contours of this knot.

For Merleau-Ponty, human experience is undeniably carnal. This carnality tears the subject in a way that faults self-consciousness. Never a self-contained entity, the body is a "gaping" wound that always remains "incomplete." The "openness" of the body is the "dehiscence or fission of [its] mass."[18] The faulty body is neither "subject nor object," neither "*in itself*" nor "*for itself,*" neither *res extensa* nor *res cogito.*[19] Rather, the body is the mean between extremes—the *mi-lieu*—in which opposites, like interiority and exteriority as well as subjectivity and objectivity, intersect. Underscoring the liminal status of the body, Merleau-Ponty writes: "At the same time as the body withdraws from the objective world, and forms between the pure subject and the object a third genre or gender of being, the subject loses its purity and its transparency."[20] In an effort to convey this elusive "third term," he uses a variety of figures and images. In addition to a "gaping" wound and "dehiscence," noted above, the body appears to be "a zero point of pressure between two solids" and "a hinge, joint, or articulation," which forms the "pivot of the world." This pivotal joint is "a being of porosity," which "is to be compared, not to a physical object, but rather to a work of art."[21] Martin Heidegger describes this association between the body and the work of art as the origin of the work of art. "Art," he argues, "breaks open an open place." The opening of art is a *Riss*—a break, fissure, cleft, gap, or tear. By holding apart what it draws together and drawing together what it holds apart, the *Riss* opens the spacing-timing through which form is articulated.[22] In some contexts, Heidegger describes the work of the *Riss* as "lighting." Merleau-Ponty then borrows the term "lighting" to describe the activity of the body. As mi-lieu in and through which subjectivity and objectivity emerge, the body is the condition of the possibility of the lighting (*eclairage*) necessary for perceptual experience. Like the tear of Heidegger's work of art, the body is the "dark hole" that allows lighting to emerge. By holding open "the open," the body creates the possibility of the play of differences that constitutes the spatial and temporal conditions of experience. The irreducible openness of the body implies the theatricality of its space. "Bodily space," Merleau-Ponty maintains, "can be distinguished from external space and envelop its parts instead of [deploying them], because it is the [obscurity necessity] in the theater to [light] up the [spectacle], the background of somnolence or the reserve of vague power against which the gesture and its aim [detach themselves], the zone of non-being *in front of which* precise beings, figures, and points can come to light."[23]

While the body always remains darkly obscure, it nonetheless has a structure that Merleau-Ponty labels "the chiasmus." *Chiasmus* derives from the Greek *khiasmos*, which in turn comes from *khiaazien*, meaning to mark with the letter χ. In grammar, a chiasmus is "a figure by which the order of words in one of two parallel clauses is inverted in the other." For Christians, χ is the sign of the cross. Merleau-Ponty develops his most complete analysis of the chiasmus in a chapter from *The Visible and the Invisible* entitled "L'entrelacs—le chiasme." An *entrelacs* (*entre*, betwixt, between; *lacs*, string, noose, trap) is an ornament consisting of interlacing figures. While *entrelacer* is to interlace, interweave, or intertwine, *s'entrelacer*, is to entwine or twist around each other. When understood in terms of *l'entrelacs*, the chiasmus figures a complex structure of "implication" (*im-pli-cation*), "enfoldment" (*enroulement*), and "envelopment" (*enveloppement*). Merleau-Ponty chooses his words very carefully to suggest the importance of a certain *folding* in his understanding of the body. In French, *plier* (to fold) is related to words ranging from *pliable* and *plexus* to *impliquer* and *compliquer.* The same associations can be discovered in English words deriving from the stem *plek*, which means bend, fold; braid, twist, and weave. Words that can be traced to *plek* include, *inter alia*, simple, complex, pleat, pliable, plight, application, comply, reply, deploy, imply, employ, complicate, duplicate, explicate, implicate, replicate, supplicate, supplement, complicity, and duplicity. It is important to hear all of these resonances in what Merleau-Ponty describes as "the structure of implication."[24]

This chiasmic structure appears so complex because it interlaces differences usually held apart in such a way that everything seems to be "completely reversed or turned inside out." Through the process of *re-pli-cation*, which in this context can be translated as "double enfolding," differences are interwoven in a relation of mutual implication that simultaneously reveals and conceals the "central cavity" or "hollow" in everything that appears to be solid. This *creux* incarnates the Heideggerian *Riss* and Derridean *différance* in the creases of the body. The "reversibility" of the chiasmus insures that neither pole in differential relationships dominates the other. Like intertwined hands that almost touch each other, the chiasmus points to "a coincidence always past or always future, an experience that remembers an impossible past, anticipates an impossible future, that emerges from Being or that will incorporate itself into Being, that 'is of it' but is not it, and, therefore, is not a coincidence, a real fusion, as of two positive terms of an alloy, but [a recovering or] overlaying, as of a hollow and a relief that remain distinct."[25] When understood in this way, the refolding of the chiasmus results in the "invagination" of differences, through which oppositions are overcome while distinctions are maintained.

> The surface of the visible is doubled up over its whole extension with an invisible reserve...and in our flesh as in the flesh of things, the actual, empirical, ontic visible, by a sort of [refolding], invagination...exhibits a visibility, a possibility that is not the shadow of the actual but is the principle, that is not the proper contribution of "thought" but is its condition, a style allusive, elliptical like every style, but like every style inimitable, inalienable, an interior horizon and an

exterior horizon, between which the actual visible is a [pro-vision-al di-vision] and which, nonetheless, open indefinitely only upon other visibles.[26]

The folds of flesh knot space and time in a way that simultaneously rends the integrity of the body and opens the doors of perception.

As the formative mi-lieu of subjectivity and objectivity, flesh clears the space in which objects emerge and perception occurs. And yet, the body is never "here or now." Forever withdrawing in order to allow appearances to appear, the body is always already past. Time, therefore, is necessarily implied in spacing. An "original past" cuts into every present to create time for spacing. The folding of flesh is the "element" in and through which spacing-timing takes place. Serra explores this element in his most recent and intriguing work.

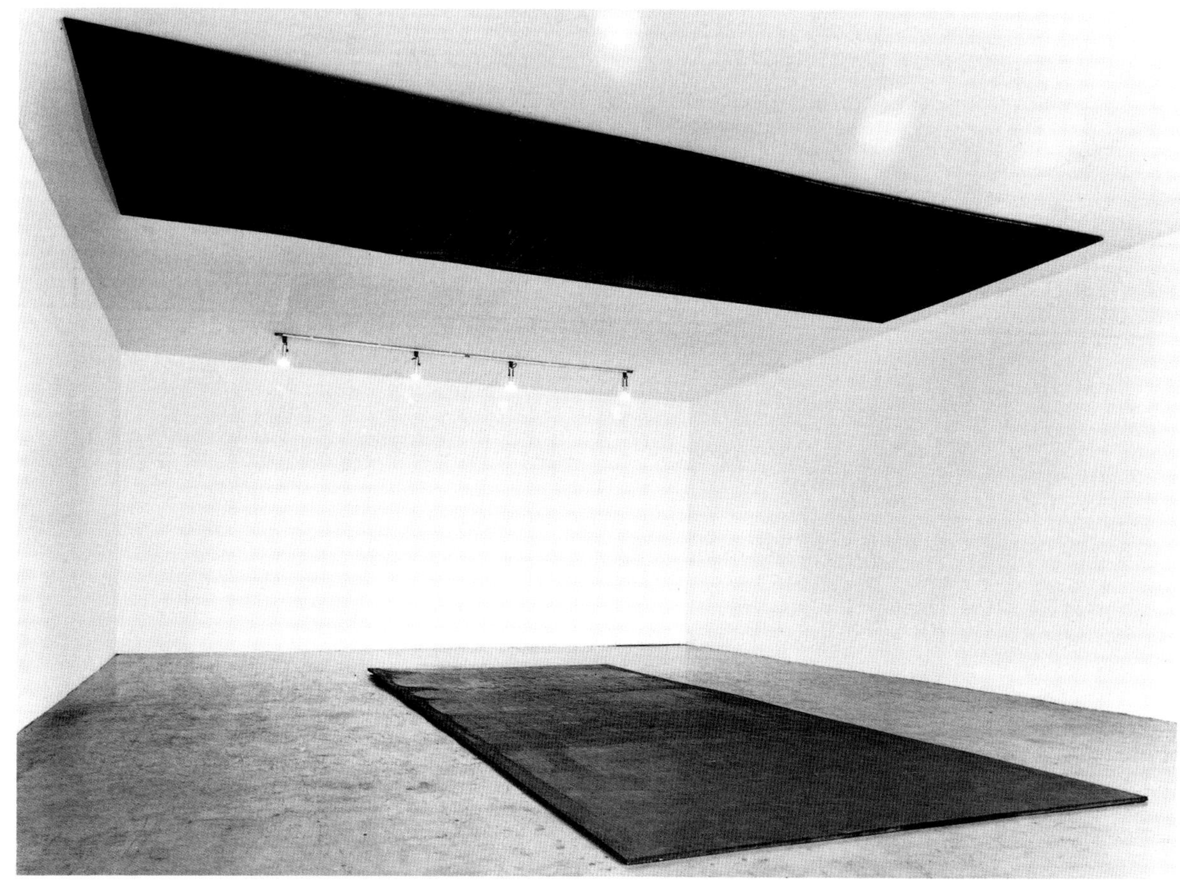

to torque

to complicate

The implicative structure of the body is further complicated by Serra's sculptural plications. Serra is obsessed with creating complex structures that enfold the body in a way that transfigures experience and thereby alters perception. This concern with experience, he insists, is what distinguishes art from philosophy and science and associates it with religion. Commenting on *Delineator* (1974–75) in an interview with Liza Bear, Serra explains:

> **RS**: The juxtaposition of the steel plates forming this open cross generates a volume of space which has an inside and outside, openings and directions, aboves, belows, rights, lefts—coordinates to your body that you understand when you walk through it. Now you might say that that sounds quite esoteric. Well, one of the things that you get into as you become more in tune with articulating space is that space systems are different from linguistic systems in that they're nondescriptive. The conclusion I've come to is that philosophy and science are descriptive disciplines whereas art and religion are not.
> **LB**: Well, they're experiential, aren't they?
> **RS**: Yes. What happens with *Delineator* is that the only way to understand this work is to experience the place physically, and you can't have an experience of space outside of the place and space that you're in. Any linguistic mapping or reconstruction by analogy, or any verbalization or interpretation or explanation, even of this kind, is a linguistic debasement, in a sense, because it isn't true even in a parallel way. (p. 36)

This is not to suggest that Serra is uninterested in conceptual issues. He is, however, convinced that conceptuality and the language in which it is articulated are epiphenomenal. Since perception—which is always bodily—is primary, the only way to change thought is to alter perception by transforming the conditions that make it possible. For such a transformation to occur, the subject—who, as we have discovered, is no longer merely a viewer—must be drawn into the open folds of the work of art.

Serra has long been interested in bending, curving, twisting, and folding. While many of his early works are rectilinear and display geometric simplicity, he has always been fascinated by the complexity of curvilinear shapes. In his 1967–68 "Verb List," he anticipates the issues to which his most recent work is devoted: "to roll, to fold, to bend, to crumple, to knot, to curve, to swirl, to encircle." The path that has led Serra to twisted materials and torqued spaces has been far from straight. For nearly three decades, he has been folding (*To Lift*, 1967; *Templet*, 1967; *Slant*

Step Folded, 1967), rolling (*Thirty-Five Feet of Lead Rolled Up*, 1968; *Double Roll*, 1968; *Slow Roll: For Philip Glass*, 1968), crumpling (*Tearing Lead from 1:00 to 1:47*, 1968; *Scatter Piece*, 1967), bending (*La Palmera*, 1982–84; *Weimar*, 1984; *W.W.1.*, 1984), encircling (*To Encircle Base Plate Hexagram, Right Angles Inverted*, 1970; *Spoleto Circles*, 1972), knotting (*Belts*, 1966–67; *Rosa Esman's Piece*, 1967; *White Neon Belt Piece*, 1967), and curving (*Waxing Arcs*, 1980; *Slice*, 1980; *St. John's Rotary Arc*, 1980) sculptural works. As straight lines and right angles give way to twists and turns, the object becomes more ambiguous and the subject's relationship to it grows more complex.

Consider, for example, the difference between the works *Strike*: *To Roberta and Rudy* (1969–71) and *St. John's Rotary Arc* (1980). In *Strike*, a sheet of steel measuring 8' x 24' x 1" extends from the corner toward the center of an empty gallery at a forty-five-degree angle. This assertive work vividly calls critical attention to the conditions of its own display. By creating "ambulatory paths" within the closed space of the gallery, *Strike* can only be grasped by "peripatetic perception." *St. John's Arc*, by contrast, is a piece of steel measuring 12' x 200' x 2fi", precisely bent to form a perfectly smooth curve. Serra moved this work outside the gallery and installed it near the exit to the Holland Tunnel. The shift of site from inside to outside and the bending of the steel resulted in a work that is considerably less assertive and more equivocal. Though seemingly simple, the *Arc* is actually exceedingly complex. As one walks around the work, it changes from a static object to something that repeatedly alternates or oscillates between convexity and concavity. Looking back on *Arc* seventeen years after its completion, Serra reflects:

> What's important in this work is not just designating the space that's made on the edge of the volume but shaping the entire space of the volume. I think the very first curved piece I built was in the rotary. It ended up being a quarter circle about 200 feet long. One of the things that really fascinated me and made me want to build it is that if you walk around, if you walk around these curves, even though they are not cylinders, you can begin to sense the difference between concavity and convexity. That's something I didn't know much about and others didn't either. The two curves involve totally different physical experiences. Now it sounds like a trite thing to say, but if something is bending away from you or something is bending toward you, your awareness of it and relation to it are as different as anything can be. That's what I wanted to investigate in the curve.[27]

With the apprehension of the duplicity of even the simplest curved object, the experience of space begins to change. This transformation grows more complex in successive works.

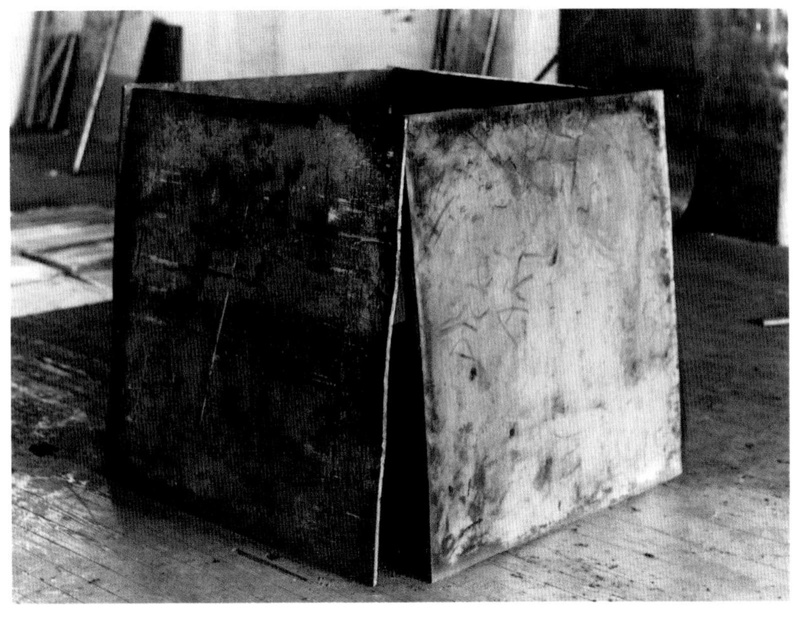

Even though *St. John's Rotary Arc* is free-standing, it appears to be stable. But this security is illusory: just as Serra sees complexity in ostensible simplicity, so he discerns instability in apparent stability. Ever since *One Ton Prop (House of Cards)* (1969) and *Skullcracker Series: Stacked Steel Slabs* (1969), Serra has been creating sculptures that seem to teeter on the verge of collapse. Pushing the object to its limit by staging a play of conflicting forces, he forges sculptures that are simultaneously massive and fragile, as well as stable and unstable. In his most famous work, *Tilted Arc*, installed in New York's Federal Plaza in 1981 but later removed, Serra extends his investigation of the "physicality of space" by slanting the arc ever so slightly to create the trace of a cone rather than a cylinder. As the vertical axis tips, the arc balances in a way that creates a sense of interiority and exteriority in a space that nonetheless remains completely open. The curve and inclining angle combine to begin the process of folding the peripatetic subject into the sculptural work.

The duplicity of the arc is further complicated when it is doubled. During the mid-1980s, Serra completed a series of works in which symmetrical arcs are positioned to create a startling range of spatio-temporal perceptions. In *Two Corner Curve* (1986), a steel arc measuring 10' x 60' x 1" is installed inside a gallery in a way that confounds the contrast between interiority and exteriority. In *Berlin Junction* (1987), two curved steel plates (13' x 42' x 2") are set at different angles to create a space that opens and closes as one moves from bottom to top and top to bottom of the work. In *Trunk* (1987), the vertical and horizontal axes of perception are confused by two vertical plates (26'11¼" x 16'8⅜" x 2⅛") that surround the body of the "viewer" like the hollow trunk of a tree. And in *Olson* (1985–86), two bent and tipped parallel concave-convex plates (10' x 36' x 2") generate a remarkable sense of vertigo. The most intriguing work in this series is *Clara-Clara*

(1983), commissioned for the entrance to the Georges Pompidou Center but installed in the Tuileries between the Jeu de Paume and the Orangerie. This work repeats and transforms *Circuit I* and *Circuit II* to create what is, in effect, a chiasmic structure. In contrast to the earlier works in which four rectilinear plates form an χ that is open in the middle, *Clara-Clara* consists of two curvilinear arcs (12' x 120' x 2") tilted at angles that create a twisted χ. *Clara-Clara*, like other sculptures in this series, is cut, torn, fissured, rent. The space-time of the work of art is the opening of the gap that forms its mi-lieu. In the midst of this between, the static becomes mobile to open space and time for the aleatory. As the duplicity of concave-convex arcs is both doubled and inverted, the complexity of the work increases exponentially. Opposites usually held apart are folded into each other to form an invaginated space where nothing remains fixed or stable and everything becomes infinitely more twisted. As space twists, nothing remains direct, clear, or simple. The spacing-timing of these plications involves a different logic, which is as puzzling as the strange logic of MA. This new logic is the logic of complexity.

Though extending the investigation of the time and space of perception that has long preoccupied Serra, *Torqued Ellipse I, II*, and *Double Torqued Ellipse* mark a new departure. These

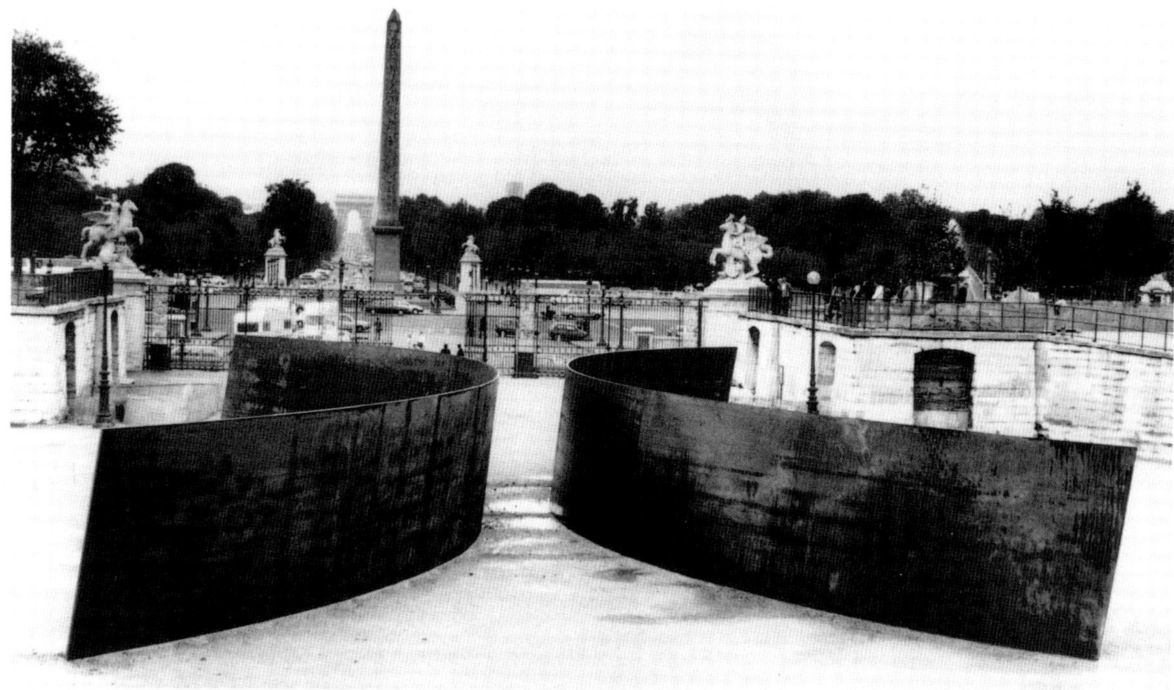

three works, which were fabricated at the Bethlehem Steel Plant at Sparrows Point in Maryland, are closely interrelated and exhibit increasing intricacy and complexity. Both *Torqued Ellipse I* and *II* are made from two steel plates, each of which weighs twenty to twenty-one tons. Serra first cut symmetrical waves along the upper and lower edges of these 15' x 40' x 2" plates and then bent them to form precisely calculated curves. Never having used their industrial machines for this kind of project, the workers at Sparrows Point initially encountered difficulties. On the first try, they broke a plate. The second time, they cracked the plate. It took more than a year to make the first piece, but the second and third were built quite quickly. The basic structure of each sculpture is the same. All the works are between twelve and thirteen feet tall and are formed by rotating parallel ellipses in such a way that the base and top are at different angles to each other. In *I*, the ellipse rotates at fifty-five degrees to itself and in *II*, the ellipses at the base and the top are at right angles to each other. The variation in the rotation of the axis of the ellipse results in different angles of incline for the sides of the work. The maximum overhang for *I* is twenty-eight inches and for *II* is five feet. *Double Torqued Ellipse* repeats Serra's gesture of multiplying complexity by doubling structures: an ellipse is placed within an ellipse to create a labyrinth of unprecedented complexity. While the bottom ellipses share the same major and minor axes, they do not have the same proportion to each other and actually form two separate shapes. The top ellipses rotate seventy degrees in opposite directions, thereby creating a maximum overhang of three feet inside and two feet outside.

The effect of these works is extraordinary. Though made of heavy industrial materials and massive in size, they have the delicacy of finely folded ribbon or even paper twisted to form a Möbius strip that never quite reaches closure. As one moves from outside to inside by passing through the gap in these works, everything shifts. Lines that appear straight on the outside bend and buckle on the inside; arcs that seem to tilt away when viewed from without bend inward to enfold subject in object when experienced from within. As twisted space surrounds or even circulates through the perceptive body, the space and time of the work of art become utterly destabilizing and disorienting.

When one enters *Double Torqued Ellipse* after having explored *I* and *II*, the effect is jarring. One encounters a dark steel wall instead of the open space of an empty center. By placing one ellipse within another, Serra creates an outside that is inside and an inside that is outside. Wedged between arcs that tilt in opposite directions at different angles, space constantly seems to expand and contract. This serpentine puzzle is deepened by the continual interplay of light and darkness. On the far end of the ellipse, exactly opposite the point of entry, a second cut appears. In this opening within an opening, space seems to move in opposite directions at the same time. Furthermore, the rate at which space moves is not constant but varies throughout the work. For Serra, this capacity to set space in motion is the distinguishing feature of his new work.

> Previously I was using the line to divide a field and declare it open. This placement of the line in relation to the understructure of the work had a lot to do with drawing. As the work became more open, the volume has become the issue. Whereas the line had defined the space, now it's the space that shapes the volume. I think what divides the work is the question of how to articulate space. But what has become the concern of the new body of work is the shape and volume of the space and your relation to it as the space actually moves. It sounds strange to say it, but the space *does* move. That hasn't happened before.[28]

By creating space that is in motion, Serra folds temporality into spatiality. The apprehension of these works of art not only *takes* time but also *gives* time a different twist. Time is no more linear than the space in which it is enfolded. In this convoluted intersection of space and time, Serra returns to the space-time he had discovered in Zen gardens.

There is, however, an important difference between Serra's youthful studies and these mature works. Attempting to formulate this difference, he explains: "Whereas in previous works, I started with materials to create the space between, in these works, I start from the void and form the object from this emptiness. In this way, the material becomes the skin of the void."[29] The distinction Serra draws between works in which materials define space and works in which space shapes volume, which is defined by materials, is as subtle as it is important. If void produces volume as much as volume produces void, then these works are, in an important sense, about nothing. Nothing, it seems, is the generative void or creative emptiness in and through which things arise and pass away. In Serra's elliptical works, everything is in motion; shapes and space are not static but constantly morph. While often baffling, this morphing is nonetheless very precise. By twisting empty ellipses, Serra torques the space that forms the "substance" of his art.[30]

This torquing of space has the strange effect of transforming objects into events. While *Torqued Ellipse I, II*, and *Double Torqued Ellipse* obviously remain static, they nonetheless create a sense of motion, which reconfigures space and time. In these works, stable objects and definitive perceptions are distant memories. Serra is more interested in processes of forming, deforming, and reforming than in structures and forms as such. For this reason, the twists and turns of his recent work more closely approximate the knotted graphs with which René Thom charts morphogenesis than the rectilinear grids of Euclidean geometry and Cartesian space.[31] The domain of morphogenesis, Thom argues, is the spacing-timing that always falls *between* form and formlessness or, more precisely, order and chaos. This interstitial site is irreducibly complex.

Not only are these works, as Serra stresses, "getting more and more complex," but they are actually *about* complexity. According to recent theorists, complexity is not so much an attribute of objects as a characteristic of events through which ordered entities emerge.[32] Such events occur "at the edge of chaos." Along this border, the systems and structures requisite for the genesis of order are open and nonlinear. Nonlinearity is a function of the bending and rebending of intricate feedback loops to form networks of exchange and transfer. Though such structures twist back on themselves, they do not form complete circles or closed circuits. To the contrary, complex systems remain open in a way that confounds the clear oppositions definitive of fixed forms. This openness issues in what Murray Gell-Mann aptly describes as complex adaptive or coadaptive systems.[33] Since complex coadaptive systems are open, they are always in the process of becoming and hence forever incomplete.

Serra's *Torqued Ellipse I, II*, and *Double Torqued Ellipse* display the openness and coadaptivity of complex systems. As space torques, object and subject fold into each other so as to subvert the opposition between inside and outside. Since outside envelops inside, which, in turn, enfolds outside, neither object nor subject is autonomous. Instead of a discrete thing, the work of art is a convoluted event that transpires *between* object and subject. The *issue* of the artwork, in other words, is as much a verb as it is a noun. The site of this work is an open field in which unfinished objects and incomplete subjects are constantly transformed in and through their complex implications.

Though his course has been far from straight, Serra has been moving toward the emptiness generative of form ever since he roamed the ambulatory paths of the Zen gardens in Kyoto. The pliable lines, bent planes, and twisted volumes of *Torqued Ellipse I, II*, and *Double Torqued Ellipse* outline the learning curves that constitute Serra's career. But the lines of his inquiry extend far beyond the objects he produces. In the openness of the space-time of the artwork, Serra's learning curves become our own. As the perceptive subject enters the work of art, the work of art enters the subject to transform perception. When perception changes, thought is recast. Since Serra's torqued ellipses are shifty events rather than static objects, the complex learning curves they trace are as infinite as the space-time they de-fine. When learning curves without ever coming full circle, it never ends.

to continue

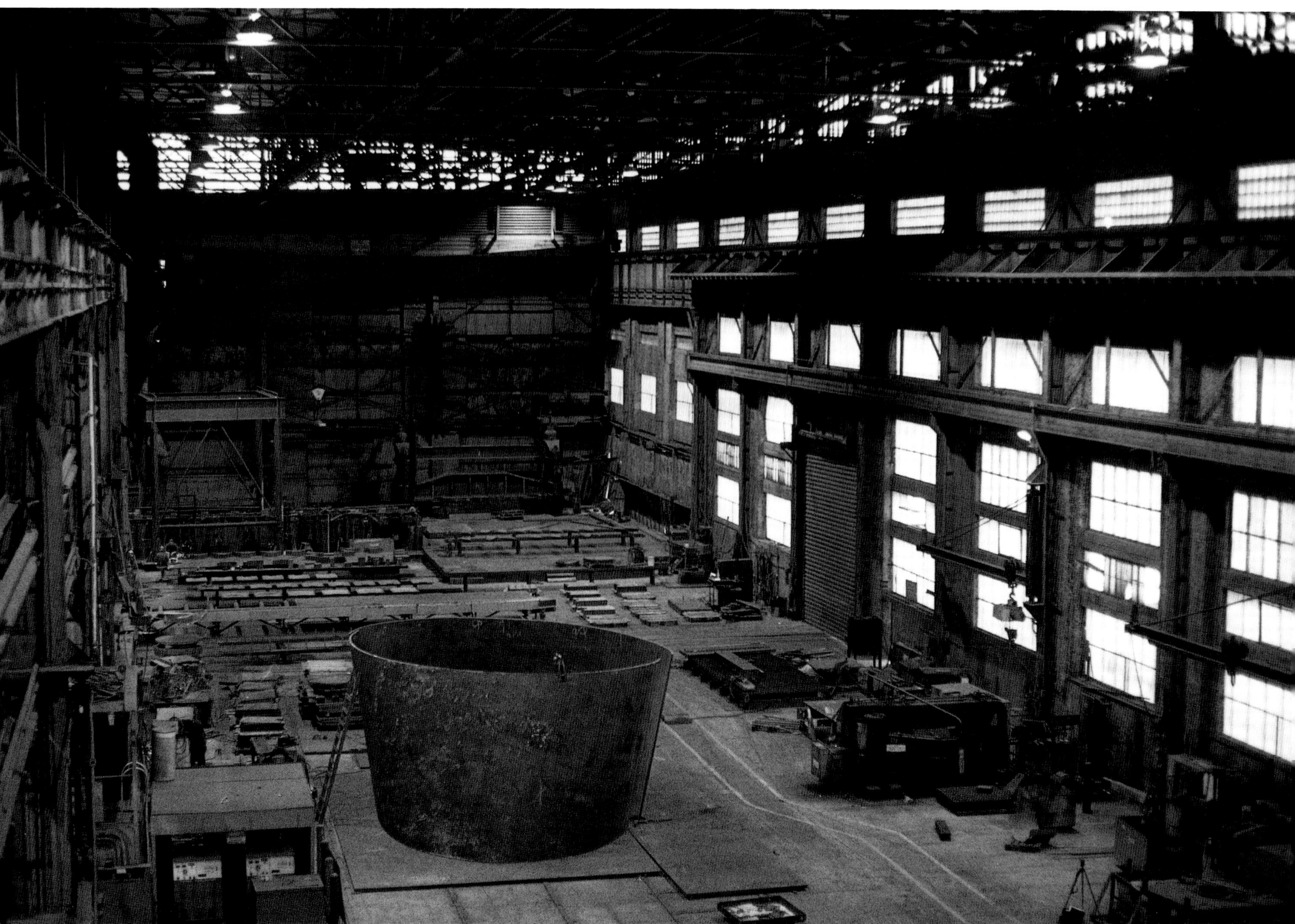

Notes

Some translations have been adapted by the author. Italicized quotations are from Richard Serra's "Verb List" (1967–68). Subtitles are by the author.

1. Conversation with the artist, 1 April 1997.
2. Interview with Lynne Cooke, in Richard Serra, *Writings, Interviews* (Chicago: University of Chicago Press, 1994), pp. 257–58. Subsequent quotes from this volume will be indicated by page numbers in the text.
3. Teiji Itoh develops helpful accounts of the history and significance of different kinds of gardens in the following books: *The Japanese Garden: An Approach to Nature* (New Haven: Yale University Press, 1972); *The Gardens of Japan* (New York: Kodansha International, 1984); and *Space and Illusion in the Japanese Garden* (New York: Weatherhill/Tankosha, 1983).
4. Conversation with the artist, 1 April 1997.
5. Arata Isozaki, *MA: Space-Time in Japan* (New York: Cooper-Hewitt Museum, n.d.), p. 13.
6. Ibid., p. 12.
7. Jacques Derrida, *Margins of Philosophy*, ed. Alan Bass (Chicago: University of Chicago Press, 1982), p. 8.
8. Conversation with the artist, 1 April 1997.
9. Rosalind Krauss, "Richard Serra Sculpture, in *Richard Serra: Sculpture*, ed. Laura Rosenstock (New York: Museum of Modern Art, 1986), p. 26.
10. Yve-Alain Bois, "A Picturesque Stroll around *Clara-Clara*," in *Richard Serra*, ed. Ernst-Gerhard Güse (New York: Rizzoli, 1978), p. 52.
11. Michael Fried, "Art and Objecthood," in *Minimal Art: A Critical Anthology*, ed. Gregory Battcock (Berkeley: University of California Press, 1995), p. 140.
12. Ibid., p. 144.
13. Ibid., p. 146.
14. Clement Greenberg, "Modernist Painting" (1960), in *The Collected Essays and Criticism: Modernism with a Vengeance, 1957–1969*, vol. 4, ed. John O'Brian (Chicago: University of Chicago Press, 1993), p. 85.
15. Conversation with the artist, 1 April 1997.
16. Maurice Merleau-Ponty, *Phenomenology of Perception*, trans. Colin Smith (London: Routledge and Kegan Paul, 1978), p. 242.
17. Ibid., p. 254.
18. Maurice Merleau-Ponty, *The Visible and the Invisible*, trans. Alphonso Lingis (Evanston, Ill.: Northwestern University Press, 1968), pp. 147, 146.
19. Merleau-Ponty, *Phenomenology of Perception*, pp. 198, 212, 80.
20. Ibid., p. 350.
21. Ibid., pp. 148, 82, 150.
22. See Martin Heidegger, *Poetry, Language, Thought*, trans. Albert Hofstadter (New York: Harper & Row, 1971), pp. 17, 72, 47–48, 63.
23. Merleau-Ponty, *Phenomenology of Perception*, pp. 100–101.
24. Ibid., p. 149. For an insightful and influential analysis of the fold, see: Gilles Deleuze, *The Fold: Leibniz and the Baroque*, trans. Tom Conley (Minneapolis: University of Minnesota Press,

1993). Deleuze's work has had a significant impact on recent architecture. See, for example, *Architectural Design*, profile number 102 (1993), issue entitled *Folding in Architecture.*

25. Merleau-Ponty, *The Visible and the Invisible*, pp. 143, 149, 123, 122–23.

26. Ibid., p. 152.

27. Conversation with the artist, 1 April 1997.

28. Conversation with the artist, 1 April 1997.

29. Conversation with the artist, 23 June 1997.

30. Conversation with the artist, 1 April 1997.

> **RS**: The pieces are getting more and more complex. Now we're putting elliptical forms inside elliptical forms to create spaces where you can walk around.
>
> **MT**: This would seem to allow you to experience space torquing.
>
> **RS**: That's what it is, that's exactly what it is! I had never applied that word to it...I think it's a good word. The space actually *torques*.

31. René Thom, *Structural Stability and Morphology: An Outline of a General Theory of Models*, trans. D. H. Fowler (New York: Addison-Wesley, 1989).

32. See *inter alia*, John L. Casti, *Complexification: Explaining a Paradoxical World Through the Science of Surprise* (New York: Harper & Row, 1994); Ilya Prigogine and Isabelle Stengers, *Order Out of Chaos: Man's New Dialogue with Nature* (New York: Bantam Books, 1984); M. Mitchell Waldrop, *Complexity: The Emerging Science at the Edge of Order and Chaos* (New York: Simon & Schuster, 1992); and John Holland, *Hidden Order: How Adaptation Builds Complexity* (New York: Addison-Wesley, 1995).

33. Murray Gell-Mann, *The Quark and the Jaguar: Adventures in the Simple and the Complex* (New York: W.H. Freeman, 1994).

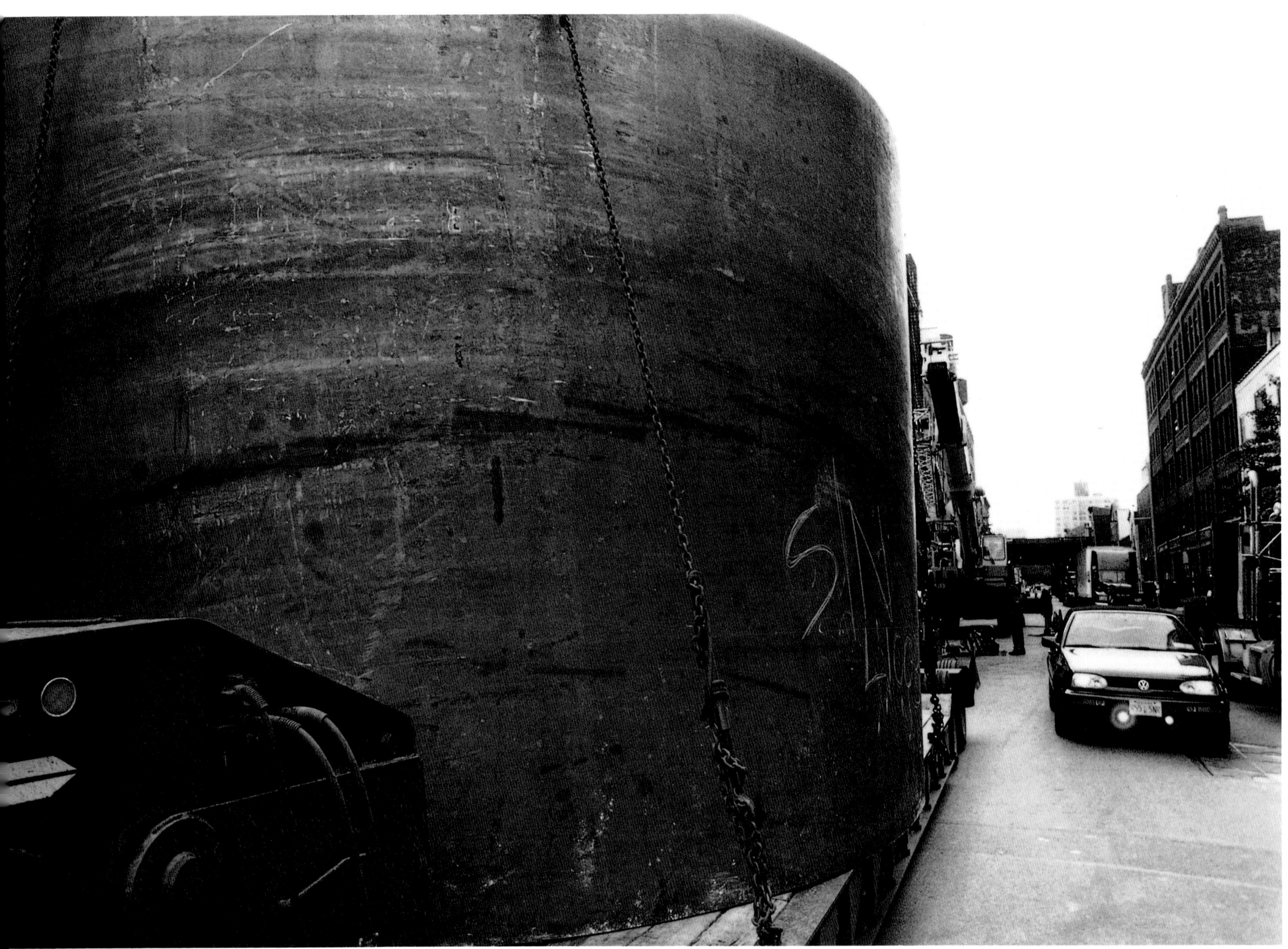

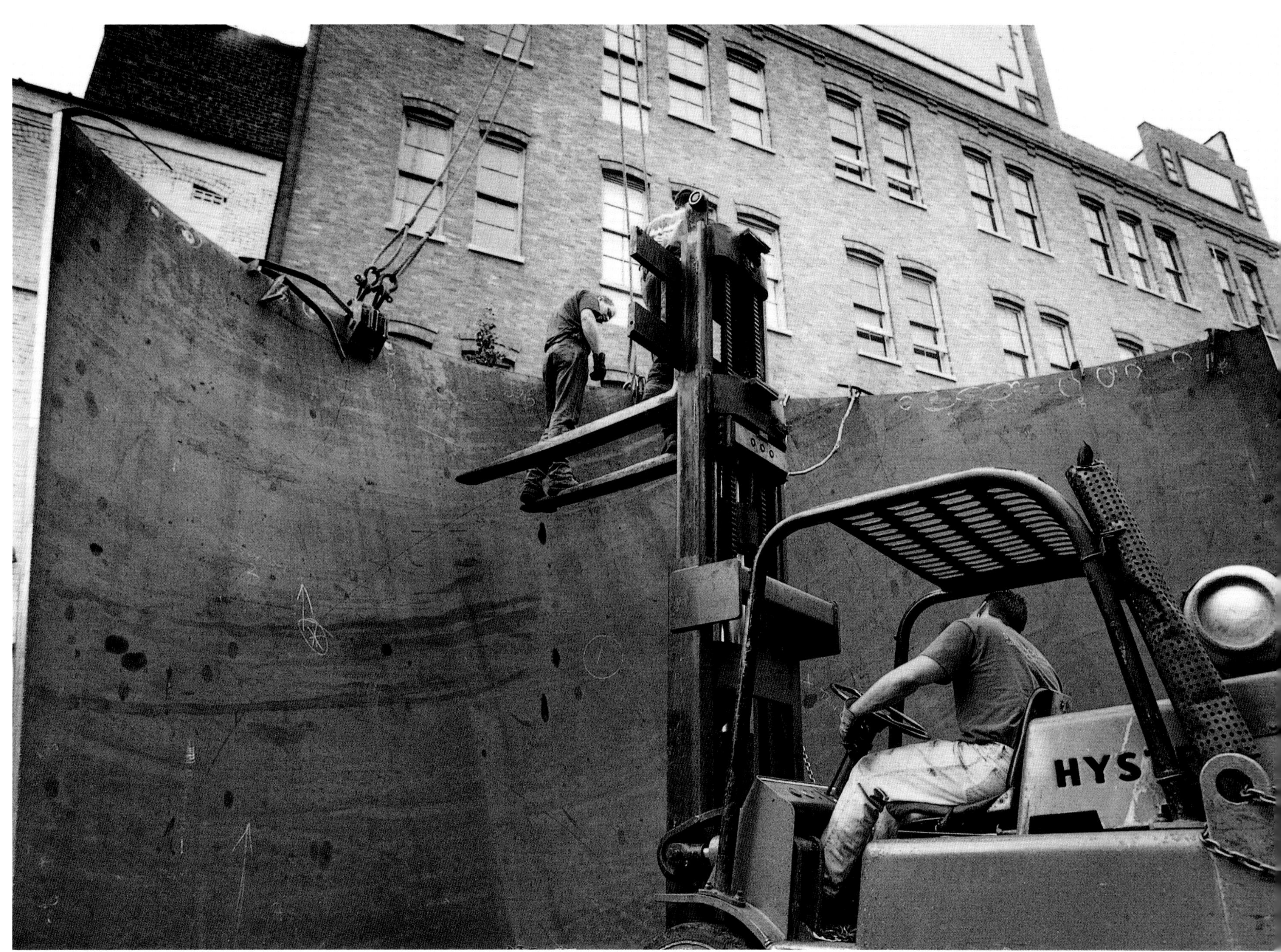
HYST

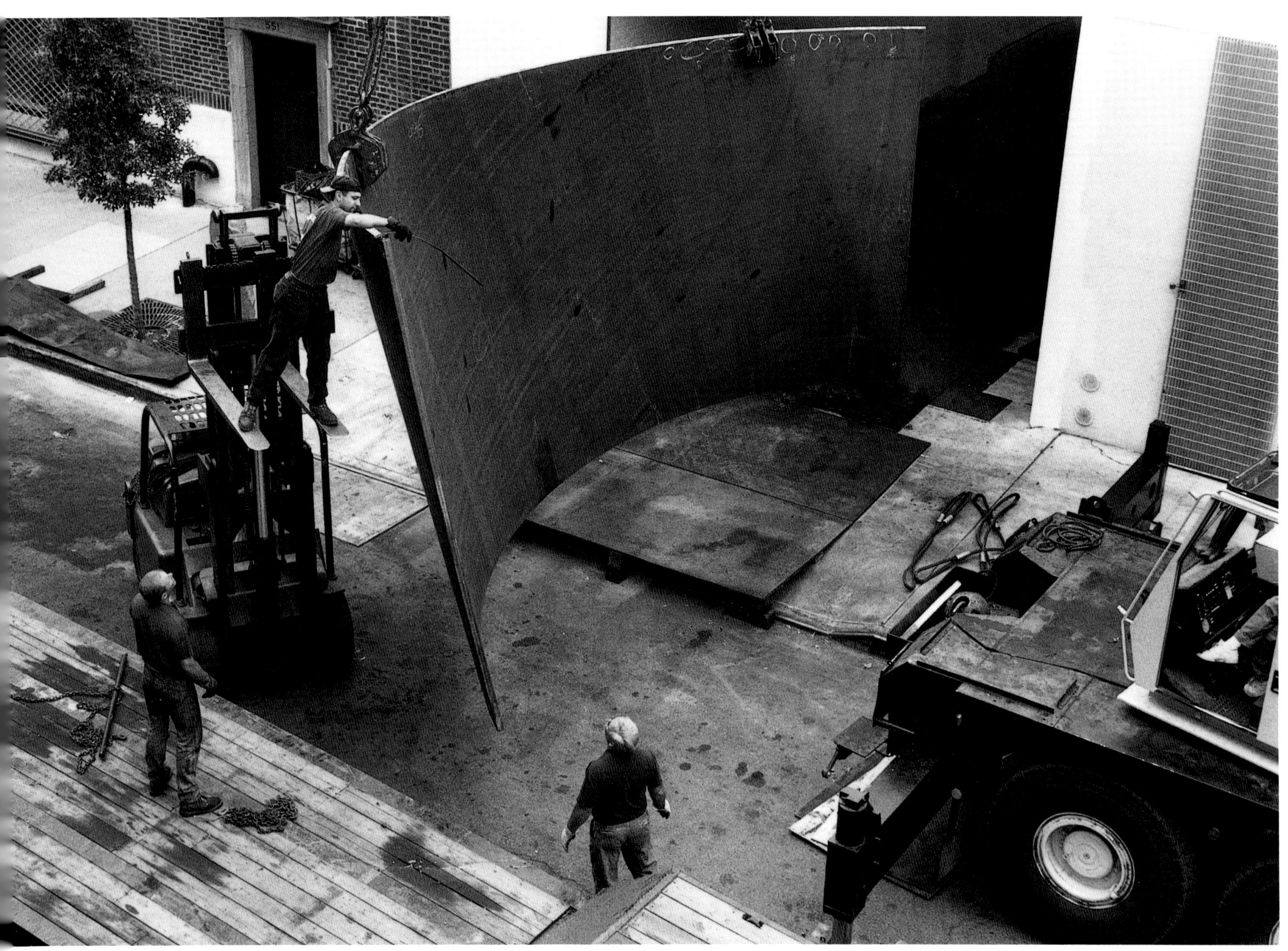
551

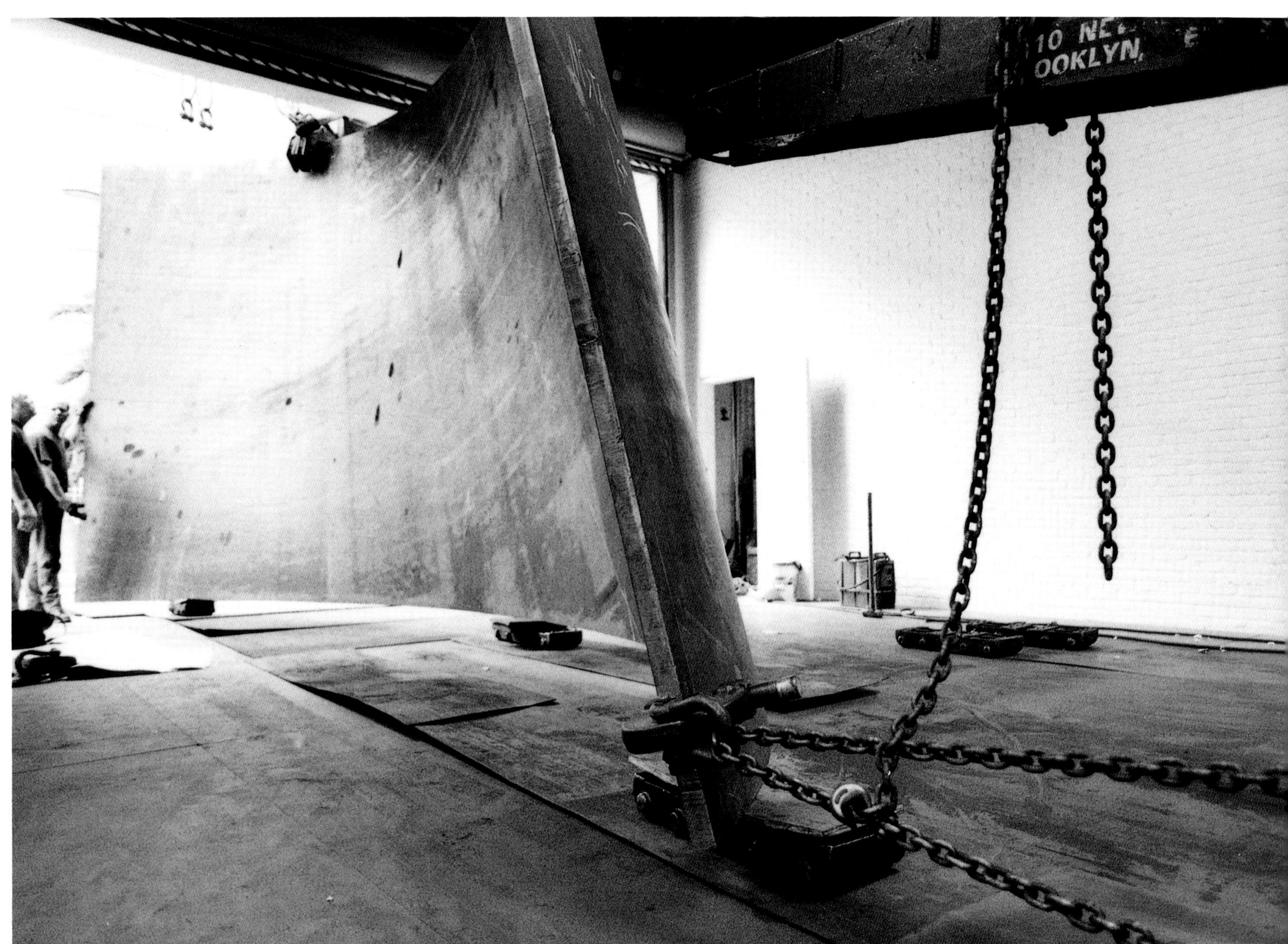
10 NE
OOKLYN,

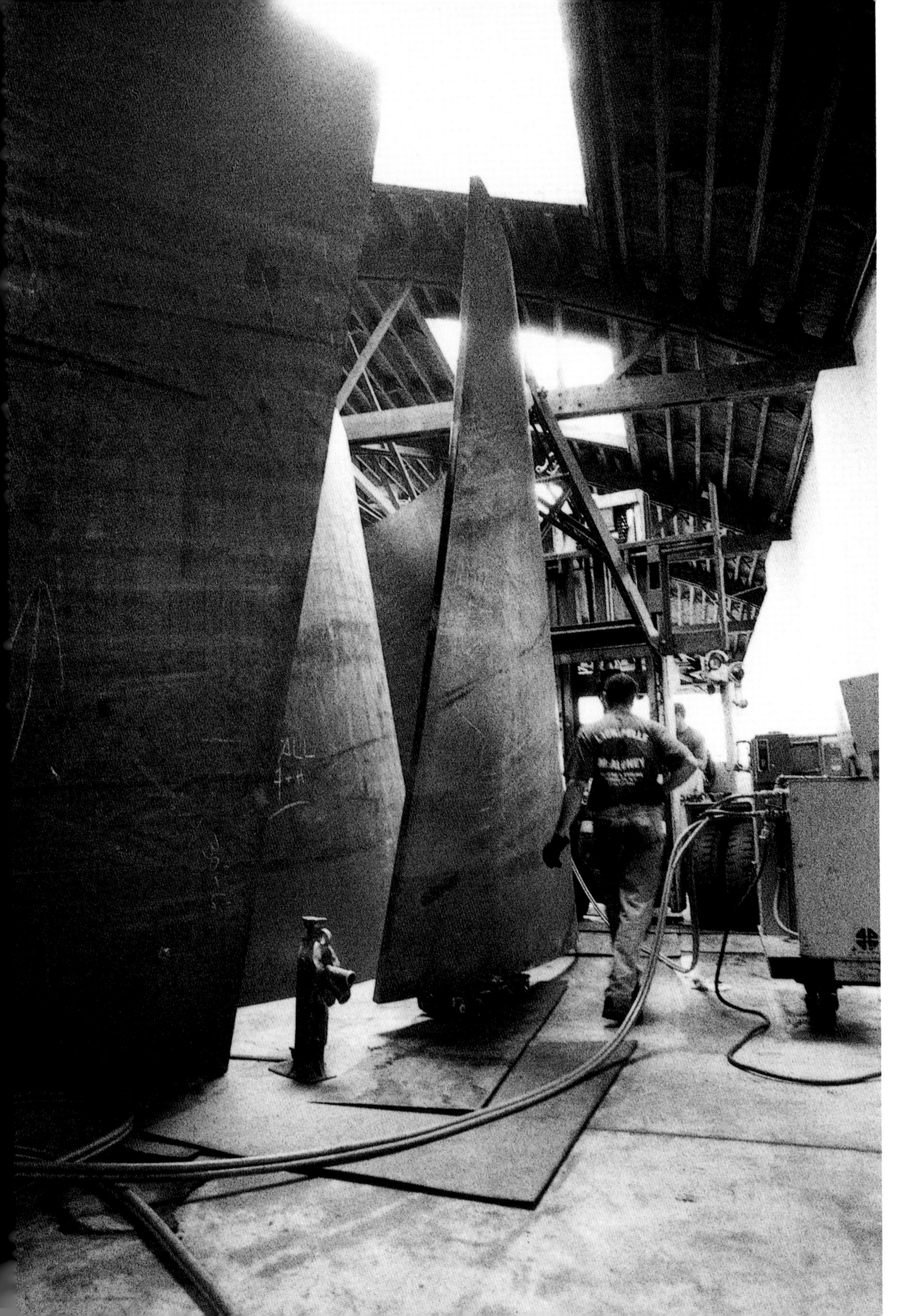

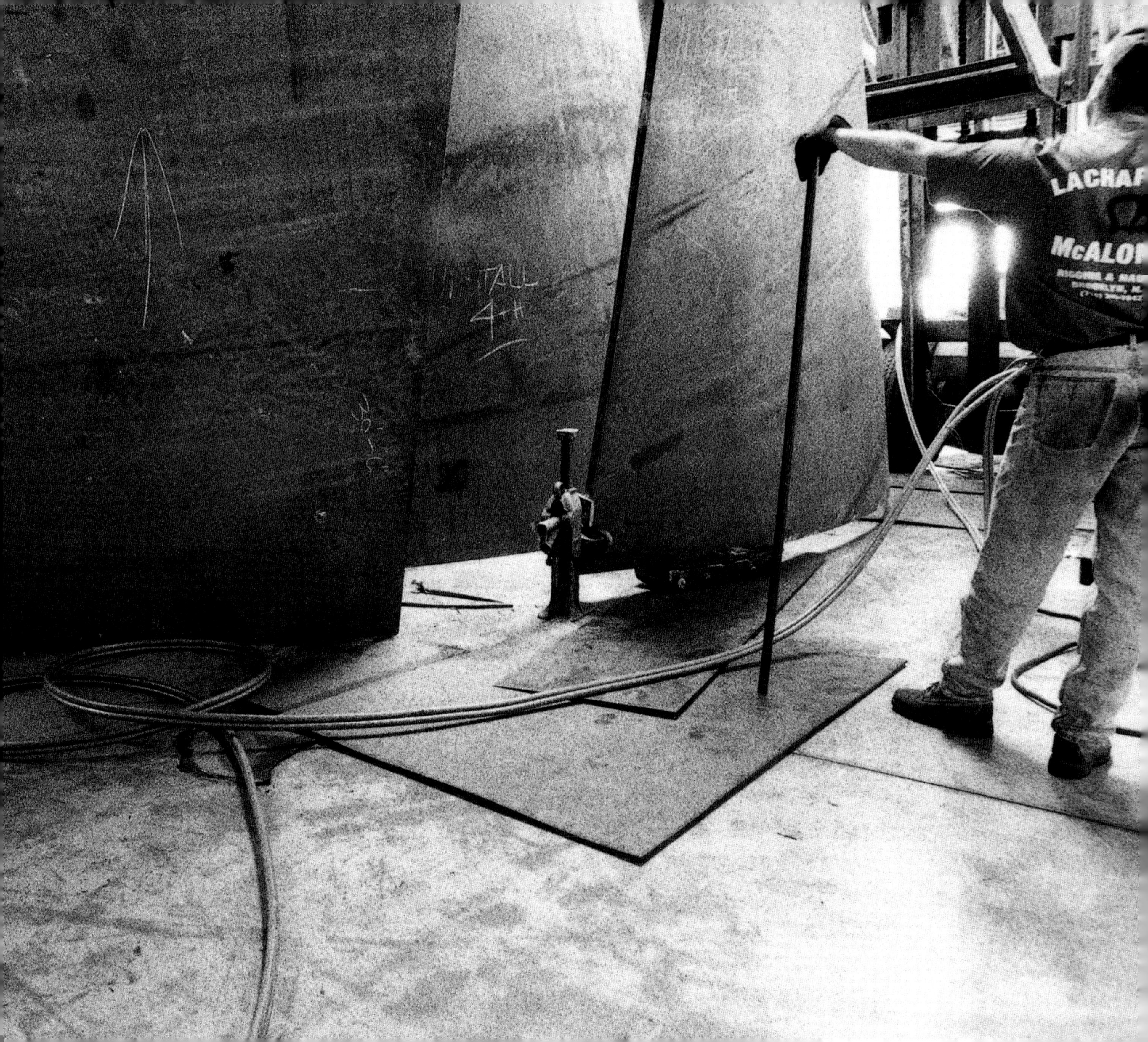

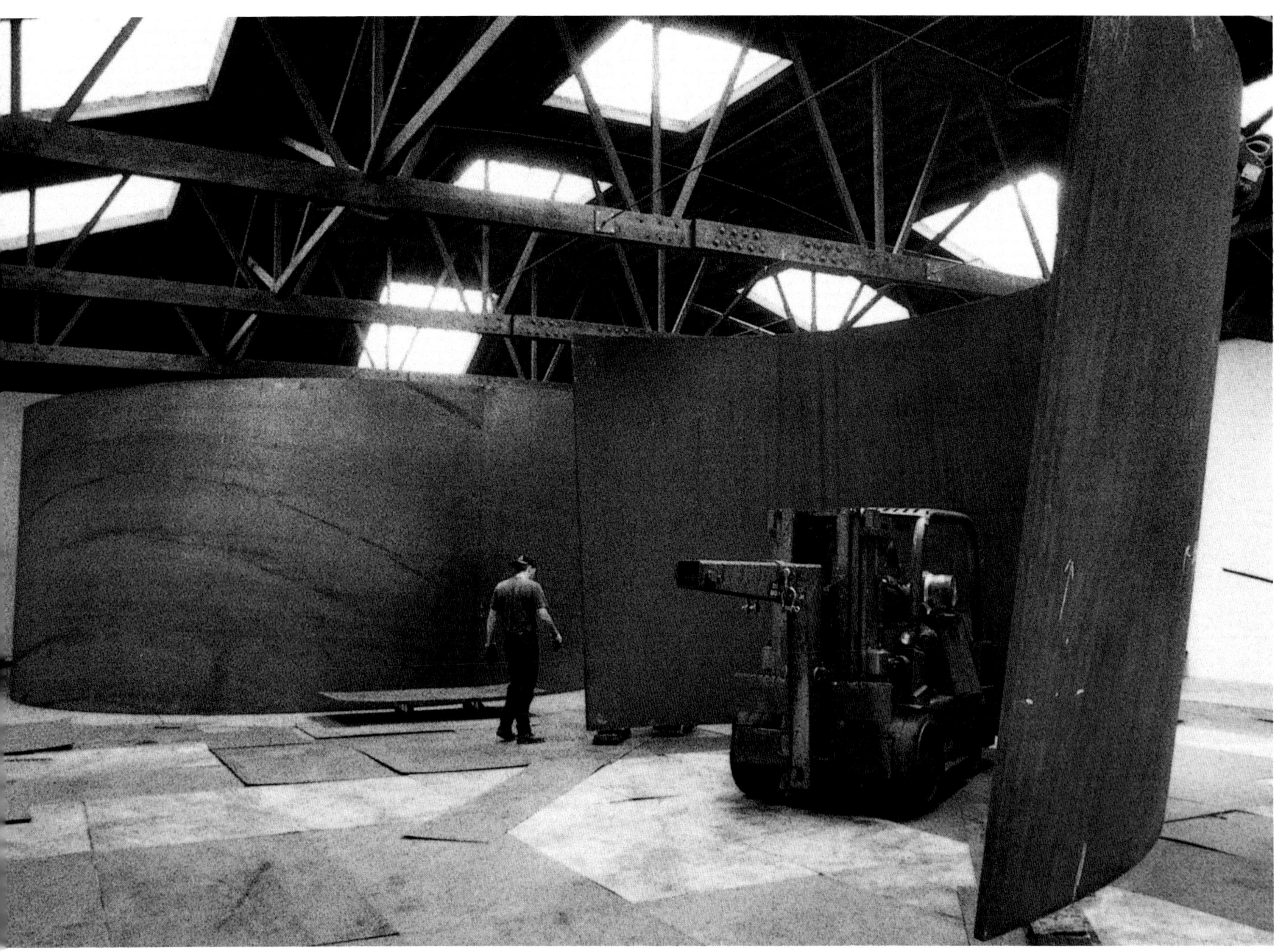

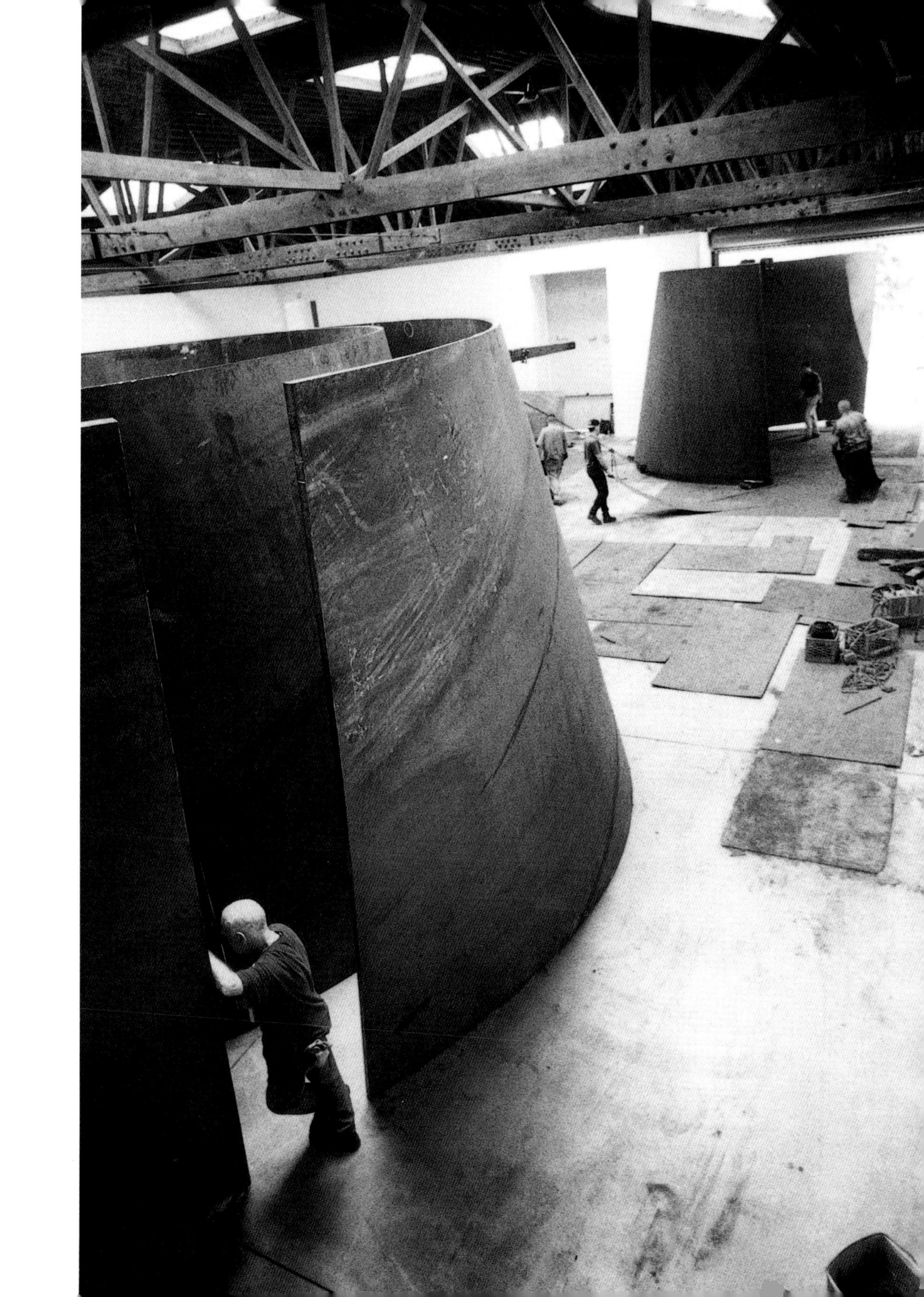

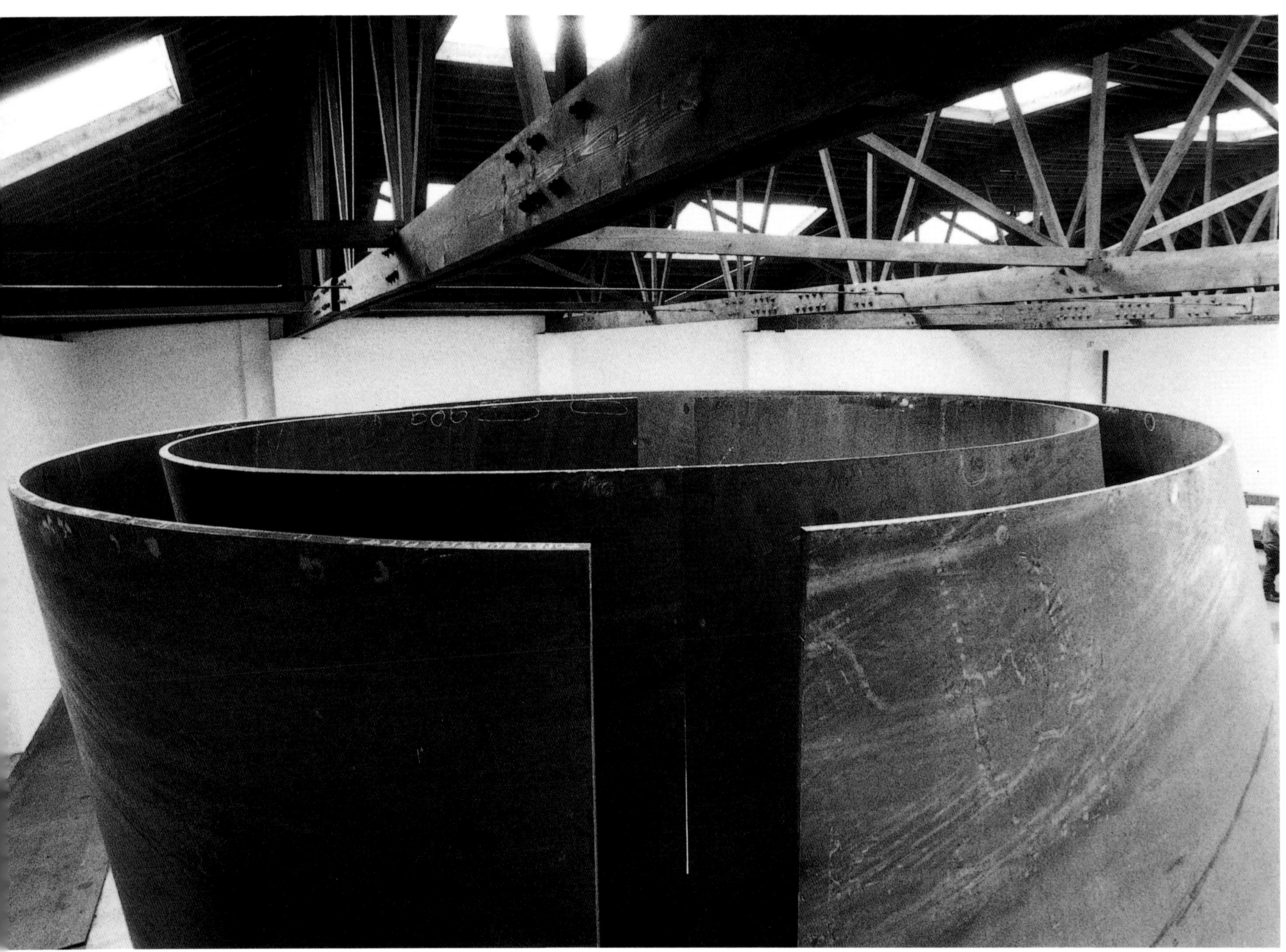

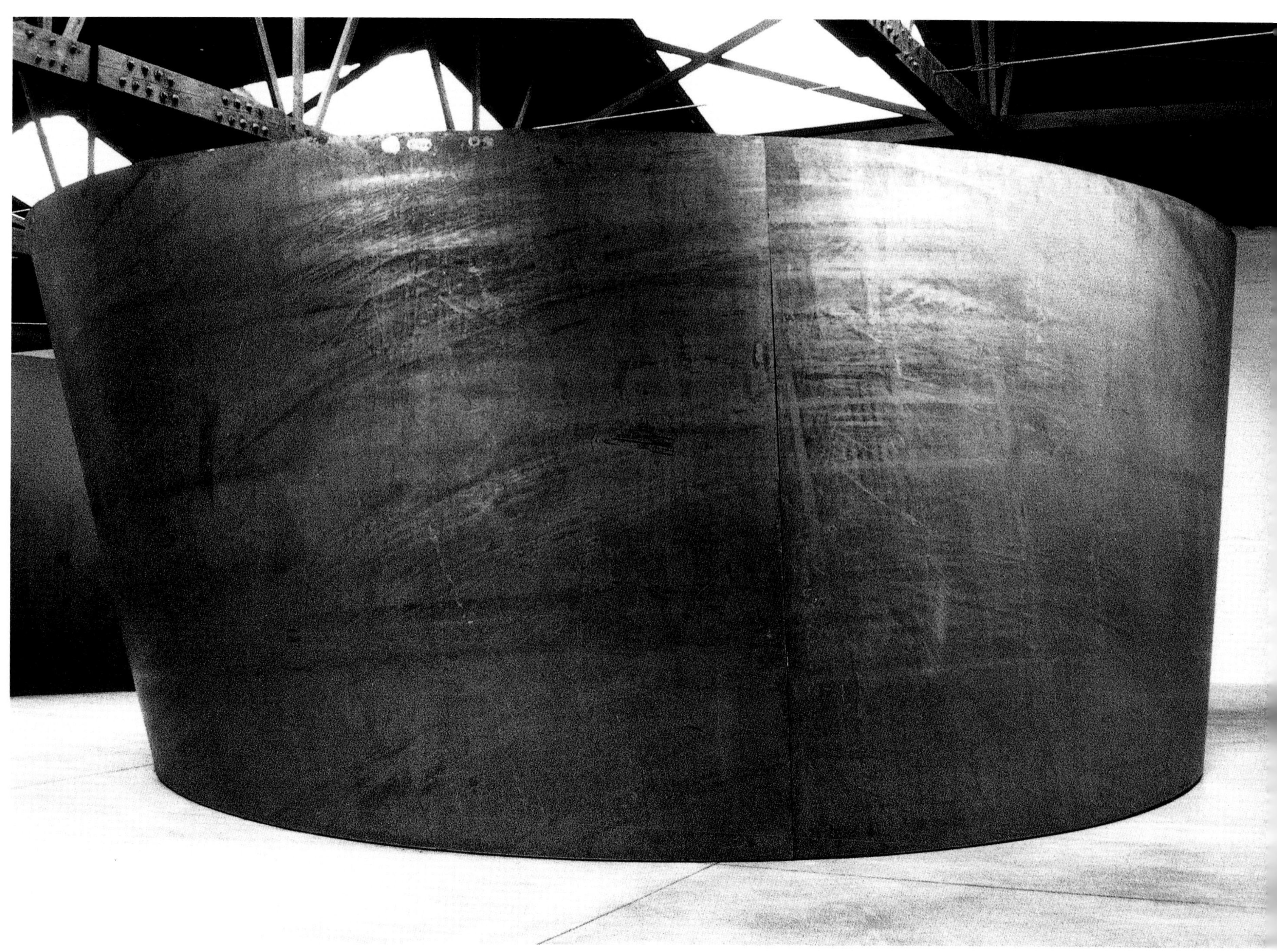

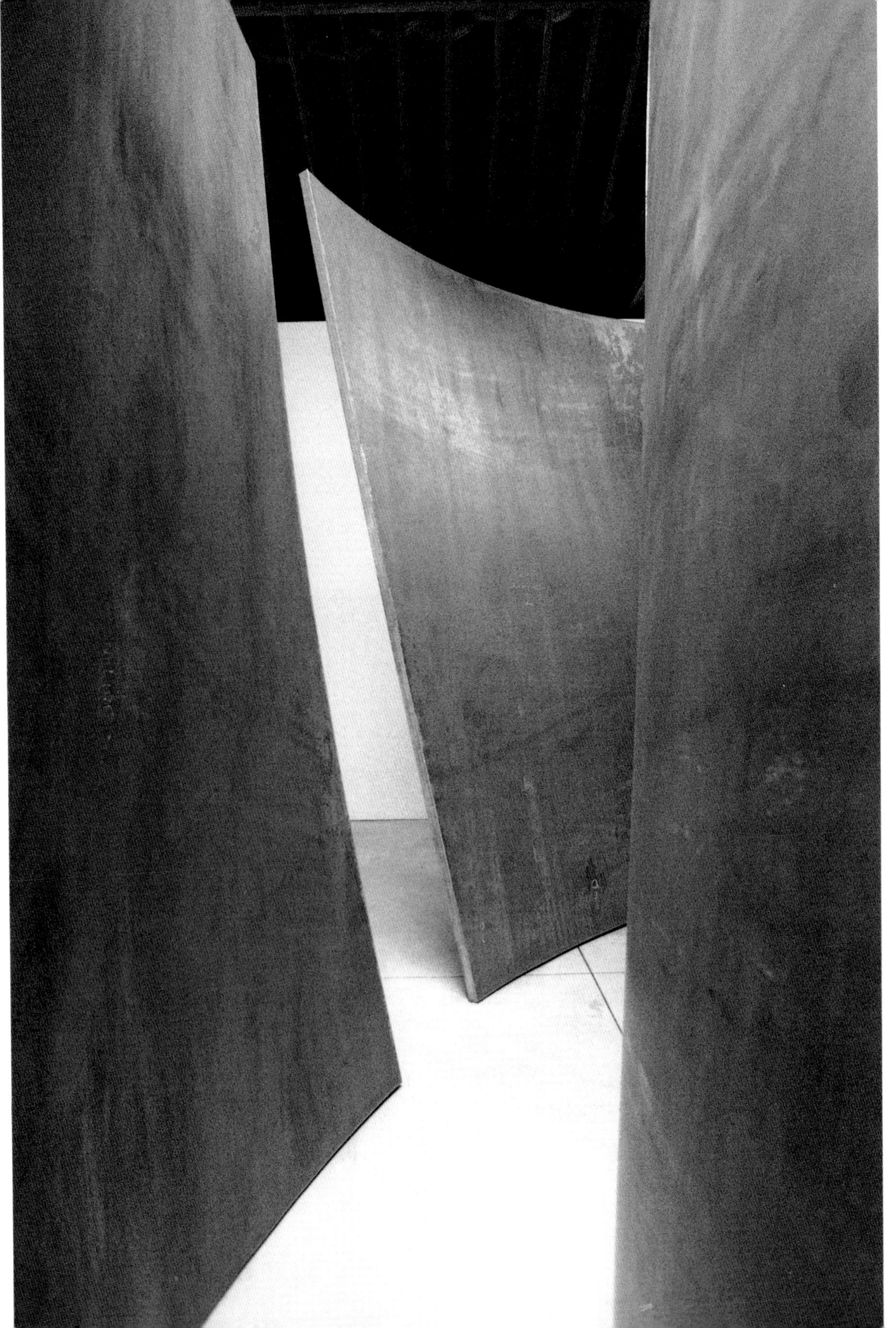

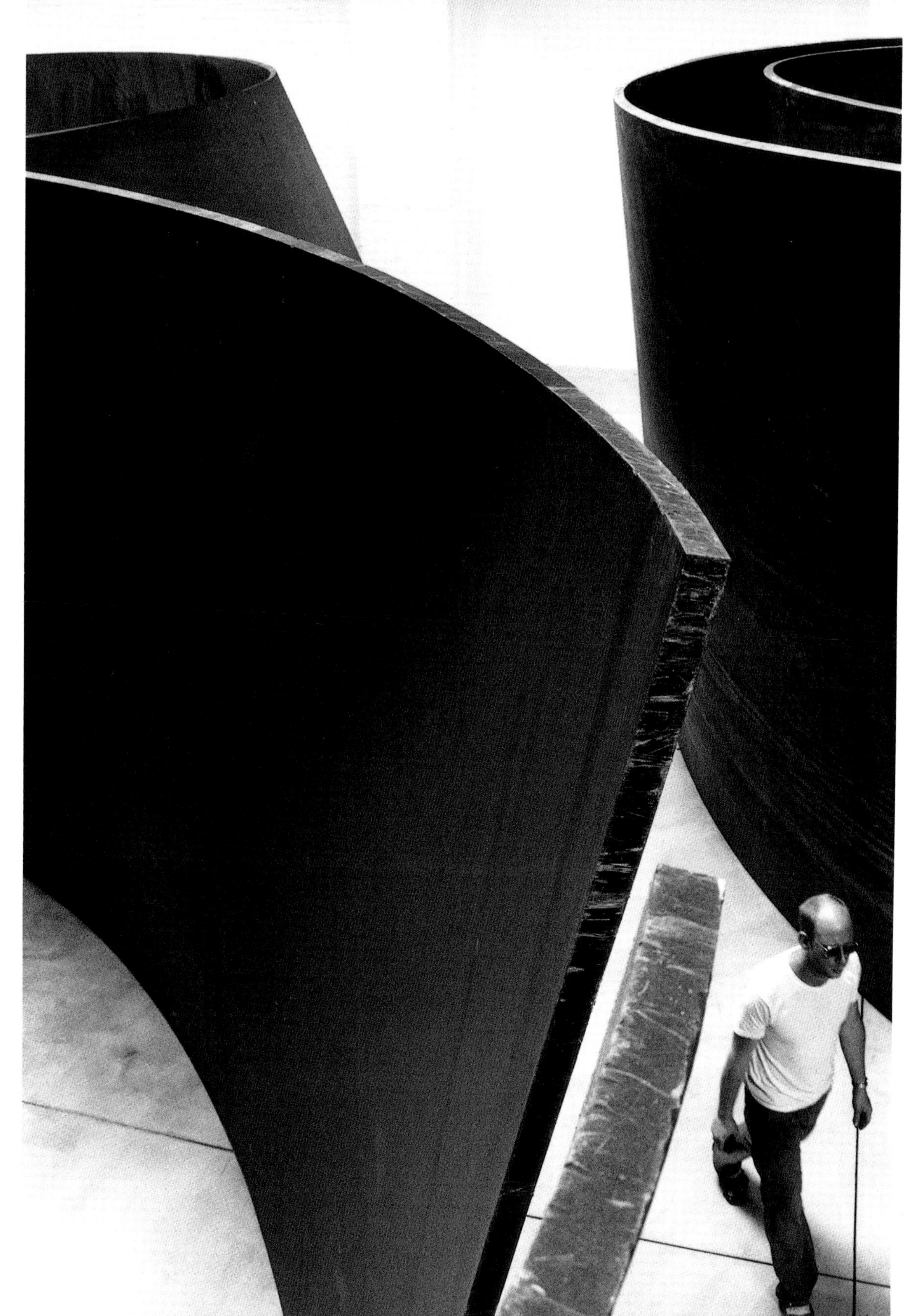

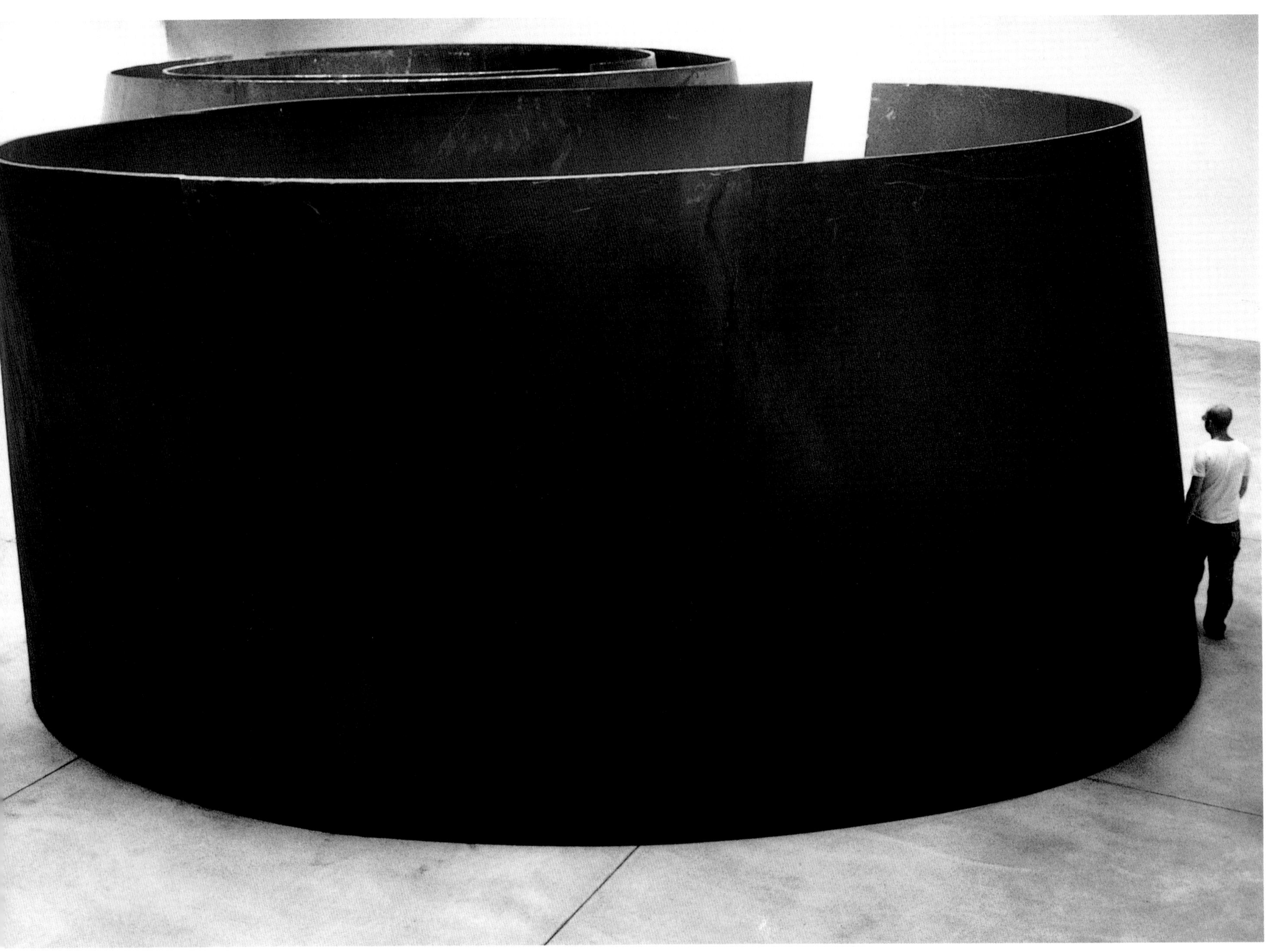

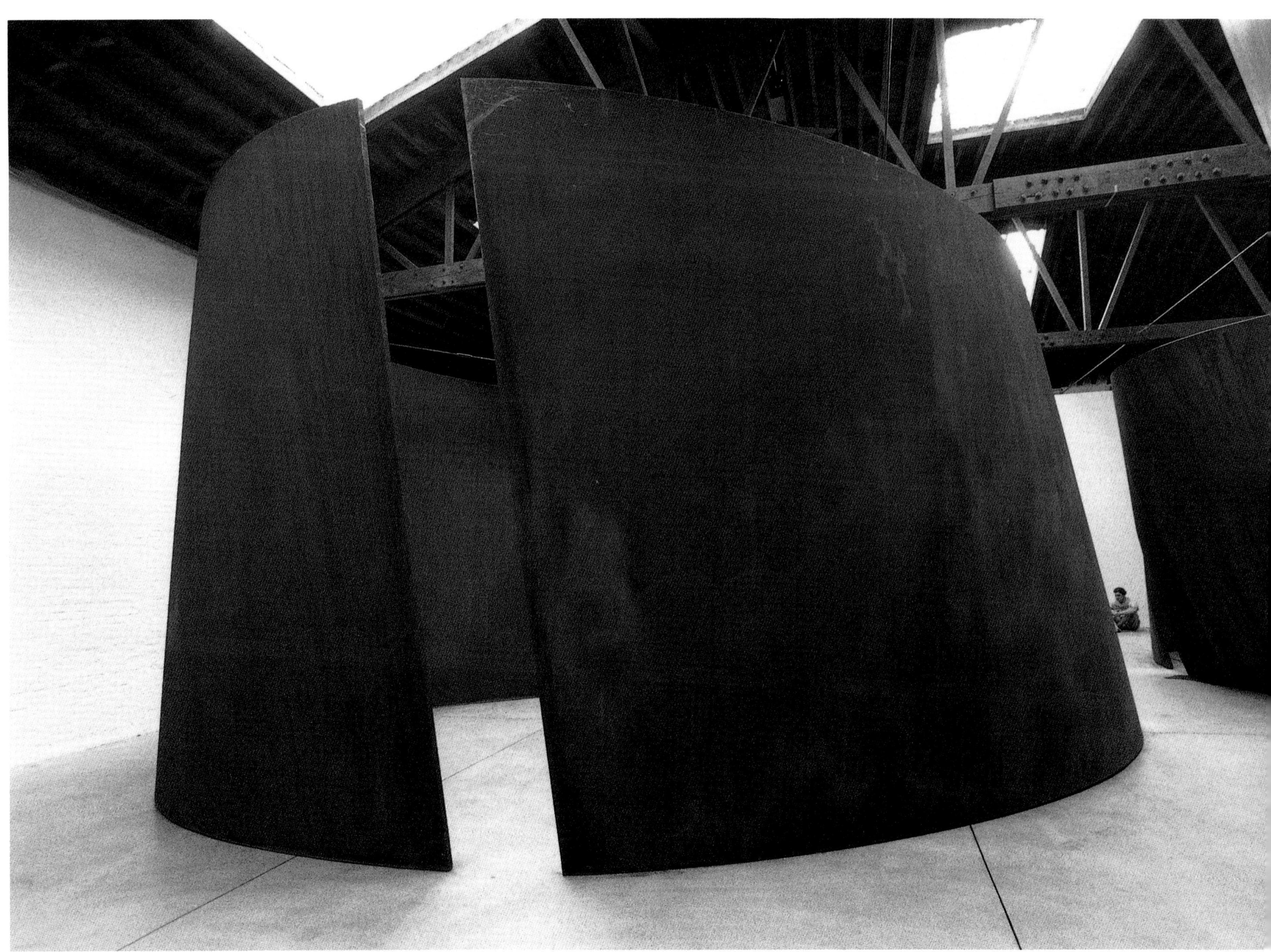

Biography

Born in San Francisco on November 2, 1939, Richard Serra studied at Yale University (1961 through 1964), where he received his B.F.A. and M.F.A. He then spent two years travelling in Europe before settling in New York, where he continues to live and work. In the following year, he began showing in museums and galleries in New York, and since then has exhibited extensively throughout the world, including a 1986 retrospective at the Museum of Modern Art in New York. In addition, Serra has created a number of site-specific sculptures in public and private venues in both North America and Europe.

For biographical information before 1986, see *Richard Serra: Sculpture*, edited by Laura Rosenstock (New York: The Museum of Modern Art, 1986).

One-Person Exhibitions Since 1986

1986

Middendorf Gallery, Washington, D.C., February 15–March 22
"Early Lead Sculptures and Lithographs," Galerie m, Bochum, February 16–May 13
"Richard Serra, Sculpture," The Museum of Modern Art, New York, February 27–May 19
"New Sculpture," Leo Castelli Gallery, New York, March 8–April 5
"Installation Drawing," New City, Venice, California, March 15–April 19
"New Drawings," Maeght Lelong Gallery, New York, March 8–April 26
"Prints," Musée de Brou, Bourg-en-Bresse, France, April 26–June 8
"Sculpture," Jean Bernier Gallery, Athens, September 25–Oct. 27
"Drawings," Louisiana Museum, Humlebaek
"Richard Serra: Major Sculpture," Hoffman Borman Gallery, Santa Monica, December 2–January 21, 1987

1987

"Richard Serra Graphics," Harcus Gallery, Boston, March 14–April 15
"Richard Serra, New Prints," Gemini, G.E.L., Los Angeles, September 9–October 24
"Richard Serra: New Editions," Pace Prints, New York, September 25–October 24
Leo Castelli Gallery and Pace Gallery, New York, September 26–October 17
"Richard Serra: Zeichnungen," Westfälisches Landesmuseum für Kunst und Kulturgeschichte, Münster, October 18–November 22
"Richard Serra: 7 Spaces—7 Sculptures," Städtische Galerie im Lenbachhaus, München, November 26–February 28, 1988
Akira Ikeda Gallery, Tokyo, November

1988

"Richard Serra, New Prints," Gemini, G.E.L., Los Angeles, January
"New Graphics," Galerie Littmann, Basel, January 1–March 18
"Zeichnungsinstallationen," Kunsthalle Basel, January 21–May 1
"Richard Serra; Lithographien und Handüberzeichnete Siebdrucke, Neuer Berliner Kunstverein, Berlin, July 1–August 6
"Richard Serra: 10 Sculptures for the van Abbe," Stedelijk van Abbemuseum, Eindhoven, The Netherlands, September 4–October 30
"Neue Arbeiten: 6 Skulpturen, 3 Zeichnungen," Galerie m, Bochum
"Richard Serra: Recent Works," Galerie Nordenhake, Stockholm
"Das Druckgraphische Werk," Wilhelm-Hack-Museum, Ludwigshafen am Rhein; traveled to: Ulmer Museum, Ulm; Graphik-Sammlung E.T.H. Zürich, 1989; Neue Galerie der Stadt Linz, 1990; Kunstmuseum Düsseldorf, 1990; Frankfurter Kunstverein, 1990; Malmö Konsthall, 1990; Provinciaal Museum, Hasselt, 1990

1989

"Richard Serra Graphik," Galerie Cora Hölzl, Düsseldorf, April 12–May 13
"Richard Serra: Gravures Récentes," Galerie Lelong, Paris, April 19–May 20
"Richard Serra: New Paintstick/Silkscreen Prints," John C. Stoller & Co., Minneapolis, May 5–July 14
Donald Young Gallery, Chicago, June 29–October 14
"Richard Serra Sculpture," Pace Gallery, New York, September 15–October 14
"Weights and Measures," Leo Castelli Gallery, New York, September 23–October 14

1990

"Richard Serra: Tekeningen," Bonnefantenmuseum, Maastricht, February 17–May 27

"The Sculpture: The Hours of the Day," Kunsthaus Zürich, March 8–April 26
"The Sculpture: Threats of Hell," C.A.P.C. Musée d'Art Contemporain, Bordeaux, June 29–October 25
"Richard Serra—Vier Neue Zeichnungen/Four New Drawings," Galerie m, Bochum, September 12–December 5
"Drawings," Galerie Yvon Lambert, Paris, October 19–November 25

1991

"Richard Serra: Drei Zeichnungen," Städelsches Kunstinstitut und Städtische Galerie, Frankfurt am Main
"Richard Serra, Malmö Konsthall," Malmö, March 23–May 5
"Richard Serra, New Editions Published by Gemini G.E.L., Paintsticks and Etchings 1991," Gemini G.E.L. at Joni Moisant Weyl, New York, September 19–November 2
"Richard Serra: Sculpture and Drawings," Gagosian Gallery, New York, November 2–January 11, 1992
"Richard Serra: The Afangar Icelandic Series," The Museum of Modern Art, New York, November 26–March 24, 1992

1992

"Richard Serra," Centro de Arte Reina Sofia, Madrid, January 28–March 23
"Richard Serra: Graphik aus den Jahren 1989 bis 1992," Saarland Museum, Saarbrücken, February 16–April 20
"Richard Serra: Drawings and Etchings from Iceland," Matthew Marks Gallery, New York, March 20–April 25
"Richard Serra: Deadweight Series," Pace Gallery, New York, March 21–April 25
"Richard Serra: Ten Prints," Susan Sheehan Gallery, New York, April 1–25
"Richard Serra: The Drowned and the Saved," Synagogue Stommeln, Pulheim, Germany, April 23–September 13
"Richard Serra: Running Arcs, for John Cage," Kunstsammlung Nordrhein-Westfalen, Düsseldorf, September 12, 1992–December 13, 1993
"Richard Serra: Weight and Measure," The Tate Gallery, London, September 30, 1992–January 15, 1993
"Installation Drawings, Richard Serra," The Serpentine Gallery, London, October 3–November 15

1993

"Richard Serra: Selections from the Permanent Collection," Solomon R. Guggenheim Museum, New York, January 22–April 25
"Serra: Intersection II," Gagosian Gallery, New York, March 13–April 17
"Richard Serra: Eight Drawings," Daniel Weinberg Gallery, Los Angeles, October 22–November 27
"Richard Serra: Wall to Wall," Benesse House, Naoshima Contemporary Art Museum, Benesse Island, October 30–May 31, 1994

1994

"Richard Serra—Props," Wilhelm-Lehmbruck-Museum, Duisburg, January 16–April 3
"Richard Serra: Weight and Measure Drawings," The Drawing Center, New York, June 3–July 3
"Richard Serra—Props," National Gallery of Contemporary Art, Warsaw, September 23–November 20
"Richard Serra: Nova Scotia Drawings," Gagosian Gallery, New York, October 22–December 23

1995

"Richard Serra: Selected Drawings," 14/16 Verneuil-Marc Blondeau, Paris, October 7–December 16
"Richard Serra: Weight and Measure Drawings," Center for the Fine Arts, Miami, October 26–January 7, 1996

1996

"Richard Serra: Weight and Measure Etchings/Ike and Tina: A Drawing Installation," Matthew Marks Gallery, New York, March 9–April 13
"Richard Serra: Drawings," Galerie Nieves Fernandez, Madrid, March 15–May 11
"Richard Serra: Prints," International Biennal of Easel-Graphic; Kaliningrad-Königsberg, September 15–November 15
"Richard Serra: 58 X 64 X 70," Gagosian Gallery, New York, October 26–December 14
"Richard Serra: New Editions," Gemini G.E.L. at Joni Moisant Weyl, New York, November 16, 1996–January 25, 1997

1997

"Richard Serra: Torqued Ellipses," Dia Center for the Arts, New York, September 25, 1997–June 14, 1998
"Richard Serra: New Drawings," Gagosian Gallery, New York, November 8–December 20 "Richard Serra," Centro de Arte Helio Oiticica, Rio de Janeiro, November 20, 1997–January 20, 1998

Bibliography

For bibliographical information before 1986, see *Richard Serra: Sculpture*, edited by Laura Rosenstock (New York: The Museum of Modern Art, 1986).

Statements, Writings, Interviews, Letters by the Artist Arranged Chronologically by Publication Date

"Answers to Zone Questionnaire." *Zone 1/2*. New York: Urzone Press, 1986.

Letter to the editor in response to Michael Brenson's "The Messy Saga of Tilted Arc is Far from Over," 2 April 1989. *The New York Times*, 28 April 1989.

"A Conversation with Sculptor Richard Serra." By M. A. Greenstein. *Artweek* 22, no. 14 (April 11, 1991), p. 20.

"Serra Interview, Richard Serra talks to Patricia Bickers." *Art Monthly* 161 (November 1992).

Text read at Tate Gallery, London 1 October 1992. *The Art Newspaper* 3, no. 23 (December 1992), pp. 22–23.

Interview by David Seidner. *Bomb Magazine* (Winter 1992).

Interview by Barbaralee Diamondstein. In *Inside the Art World*. By Barbaralee Diamondstein. New York: Rizzoli International, 1994.

"Happy Birthday Jorge Orteiza." *El Diario Vasco* (San Sebastian) Supplemento Especial, 21 October 1993.

"Richard Serra: Schusselerbnis in der Weft." Interview by Victor Weber. *Basler Zeitung*, 19 January 1994, p. 23.

"Some Aspects of Color in Red and Black in Particular." *Artforum* 32, no. 10 (Summer 1994), pp. 70, 113–114.

"Cy Twombly: An Artist's Artist." Discussion with Kirk Varnedoe, Francesco Clemente, Brice Marden on 4 October 1994 on the occasion of Twombly retrospective at the Museum of Modern Art, New York. *Res* 28 (1995), pp. 161–79.

Books, Catalogues for One-Person Exhibitions, Monographs Arranged Chronologically

Richard Serra: Sculpture. Edited by Laura Rosenstock. New York: The Museum of Modern Art, 1986. Texts by Douglas Crimp and Rosalind E. Krauss.

Public Art, Public Controversy: The Tilted Arc on Trial. New York: American Council on the Arts, 1987.

Richard Serra: Sculpture 1985–1987. New York: Leo Castelli Gallery/Pace Gallery, 1987.

Richard Serra at Gemini 1983–1987. Los Angeles: Gemini GEL, 1988.

Richard Serra: Neue Skulpturen in Europa 1986–1988. Bochum: Galerie m, 1988. Text by Richard Serra.

Richard Serra's Tilted Arc. Edited by Clara Weyergraf and Martha Buskirk. Eindhoven: Stedeljik Van Abbemuseum, 1988.

Das druckgraphische Werk, Prints–A Catalogue Raisonné, 1972–1988. Bochum: Galerie m, 1988. Text by Richard Hoppe-Sailer.

Richard Serra. 10 Sculptures for the Van Abbe. Eindhoven: Stedeljik Van Abbemuseum, 1988.

Richard Serra. Edited by Ernst-Gerhard Güse. Stuttgart: Verlag Gerd Hatje, in association with Westfälisches Landesmuseum für Kunst und Kulturgeschichte, Münster, 1987. English edition: New York: Rizzoli International, 1988. Texts by Jean-Christophe Ammann, Yve-Alain Bois, Douglas Crimp, Ernst-Gerhard Güse, Armin Zweite. English version includes text by Richard Serra.

Richard Serra Sculpture 1987–1989. New York: Pace Gallery, 1989. Text by Richard Serra.

Richard Serra: "Maillart Extended." Bern: Benteli Verlag, 1989. Interview by Harald Szeemann.

Richard Serra. Zürich: Kunsthaus Zürich, 1990. Texts by Harald Szeemann and Stefan Germer.

Richard Serra, Drawings, Zeichnungen 1969–90. Catalogue Raisonné. Bonnefantenmuseum, Maastricht. Edited by Hans Janssen. Bern: Benteli Verlag, 1990. Texts by Yve-Alain Bois and Richard Serra.

Richard Serra, Interviews, Schriften, 1970–89. Edited by Harald Szeemann. Bern: Benteli Verlag, 1990.

Richard Serra: Ecrits et entretiens 1970–89. Edited by Daniel Lelong. Paris: Galerie Lelong, 1990.

Richard Serra: Axis Dokumentation. Bielefeld: Kunsthalle, 1990.

The Destruction of Tilted Arc: Documents. Edited by Clara Weyergraf and Martha Buskirk. Cambridge, Mass.: The MIT Press, 1991.

Richard Serra: "Octagon for Saint Eloi." Paris: Déléguéaux Arts Plastiques au Ministère de la Culture et la Communication, 1991.

Afangar. Gottingen: Steidl Verlag and Parkett Publishers, Zürich, 1991. Drawings by Richard Serra. Photographs by Dirk Reinartz.

Richard Serra: Drawings and Etchings from Iceland. New York: Matthew Marks Gallery, 1992. Interview by Mark Rosenthal.

Richard Serra: "Running Arcs, for John Cage." Düsseldorf: Richter Verlag, in association with Kunstsammlung Nordrhein-Westfalen, 1992. Text by Armin Zweite.

Richard Serra Deadweight Series. New York: Pace Gallery, 1992.

Richard Serra Gravures. Céret: Musée d'Art Moderne de Céret, 1992. Text by Christine Buci Glucksmann.

Richard Serra: "Weight and Measure." Düsseldorf: Richter Verlag, in association with The Tate Gallery, London, 1992. Interview with Nicholas Serota and David Sylvester.

Richard Serra: Installation Drawings. Düsseldorf: Richter Verlag, in association with The Serpentine Gallery, London 1992. Interview with Lynne Cooke, text by Richard Serra.

Richard Serra. Madrid: Museo Nacional Reina Sofia, 1992. Texts by Richard Serra, Yve-Alain Bois, Stefan Germer.

Richard Serra: "The Drowned and the Saved." Pulheim: Synagogue Stommeln, 1992. English version: New York: Matthew Marks Gallery, 1992. Statement by Richard Serra. English version includes text by Stefan Germer.

Richard Serra: Afangar Icelandic Series, 1988–1992. Los Angeles: Gemini GEL, 1992. Statement by Richard Serra.

Richard Serra. By Alfred Pacquement. Paris: Jalons, in association with Musée National d'Art Moderne et du Centre de Creation Industrielle, 1993.

Torque: Dokumentation zu der Grosskulptur auf der Universitat des Saarlandes. Edited by Uwe Loebens. Saarbrucken: St. Johann Verlag, in association with Institut für aktuelle Kunst, 1993.

Richard Serra: Props. The Wilhelm Lehmbruck Museum. Düsseldorf: Richter Verlag, 1994. Acceptance of Lehmbruck Award by Richard Serra. Text by Rosalind Krauss.

Richard Serra. Warsaw: National Gallery of Contemporary Art, 1994. Text by Rosalind Krauss.

Richard Serra: Nova Scotia Drawings. New York: Gagosian Gallery, 1994. Text by Michael Brenson.

Richard Serra: Weight and Measure Drawings. New York: The Drawing Center, 1994. Texts by Dave Hickey and Richard Shiff.

Richard Serra: Writings, Interviews. Chicago: The University of Chicago Press, 1994.

Richard Serra: Drawings and Prints. Osaka: The National Museum of Art, 1994.

Der Liebhafte Raum: das Terminal von Richard Serra in Bochum. By Karen van den Berg. Ostfildern: Edition Tertium.

Richard Serra, Exchange Luxembourg. Luxembourg: Musée Nationale d'Histoire et d'Art, 1996. Text by Lucien Kayser. Interview by Enrico Lunghi.

Intersection: Richard Serra. Düsseldorf: Richter Verlag, 1996.

La Mormaire: Richard Serra, Dirk Reinartz. Edited by Alexander von Berswordt. Düsseldorf: Richter Verlag, 1997. Text by Stefan Germer.

Photo Credits

cover photograph by Dirk Reinartz

pages 10, 14–16, 18, 21, 24, 25, 57, and 79
photographs of the models of Torqued Ellipses and during their construction at Beth Ship, Maryland, by Dirk Reinartz

pages 60–68
photographs of the Torqued Ellipses during installation at Dia Center for the Arts by Ken Goebel

pages 30, 31, 69–73
photographs of the Torqued Ellipses installed at Dia Center for the Arts by Ivory Serra

page 11
Intersection, 1993
Cor-Ten steel
12' x 42' x 25'8" x 2"
collection of City of Basel
photograph by Dirk Reinartz

page 12
model of Torqued Ellipses
photograph by Ivory Serra

page 12
CATIA computer drawings
courtesy Rick Smith

page 23
To Lift, 1967
vulcanized rubber
3' x 6'8"
courtesy of the artist
photograph by Peter Moore

page 26
58 x 64 x 70, 1996
forged steel
6 blocks: 4'10" x 5'4" x 5'10"
installation at Gagosian Gallery, New York
courtesy of the artist and Gagosian Gallery, New York
photograph by Dirk Reinartz

page 28
Pulitzer Piece: Stepped Elevation, 1971
Cor-Ten steel
three plates:
5" x 40'3" x 2"
5" x 45' x 11" x 2"
5" x 50'7" x 2"
collection of Mr. and Mrs. Joseph Pulitzer, Jr., St. Louis

page 29
Snake Eyes and Boxcars, 1993
forged steel
6 blocks, each 7' x 3'5" x 3'5"
installation in Geyserville, California
collection of Steve Oliver
photograph by Dirk Reinartz

page 38
Circuit, 1972
hot rolled steel
four plates, each 8' x 24' x 1"
installed 8' x 36' x 36'
temporary installation at documenta 5, Kassel, 1972
collection of The Museum of Modern Art, New York

page 39
Shift, 1970–72
concrete
six sections:
5' x 90' x 8"
5' x 240' x 8"
5' x 150' x 8"
5' x 120' x 8"
5' x 105' x 8"
5' x 110' x 8"
The hill's elevational fall determines each part's outline and length.
installation in King City, Ontario
collection of Roger Davidson, Toronto

page 49
Delineator, 1974–76
steel
two plates, each 10' x 26'
installation at Ace Gallery, Venice, California
collection of Lembachhaus Munich
photograph by Flow Ace Gallery

page 52
One-Ton Prop (House of Cards), 1969
lead antimony
four plates, each 4' x 4'
collection of the Museum of Modern Art, New York
photograph by Peter Moore

page 53
Clara-Clara, 1983
Cor-Ten steel
two elements, each 12' x 120' x 2"
installation at Jardin des Tuilleries, Paris
collection of the City of Paris
photograph by Dirk Reinartz

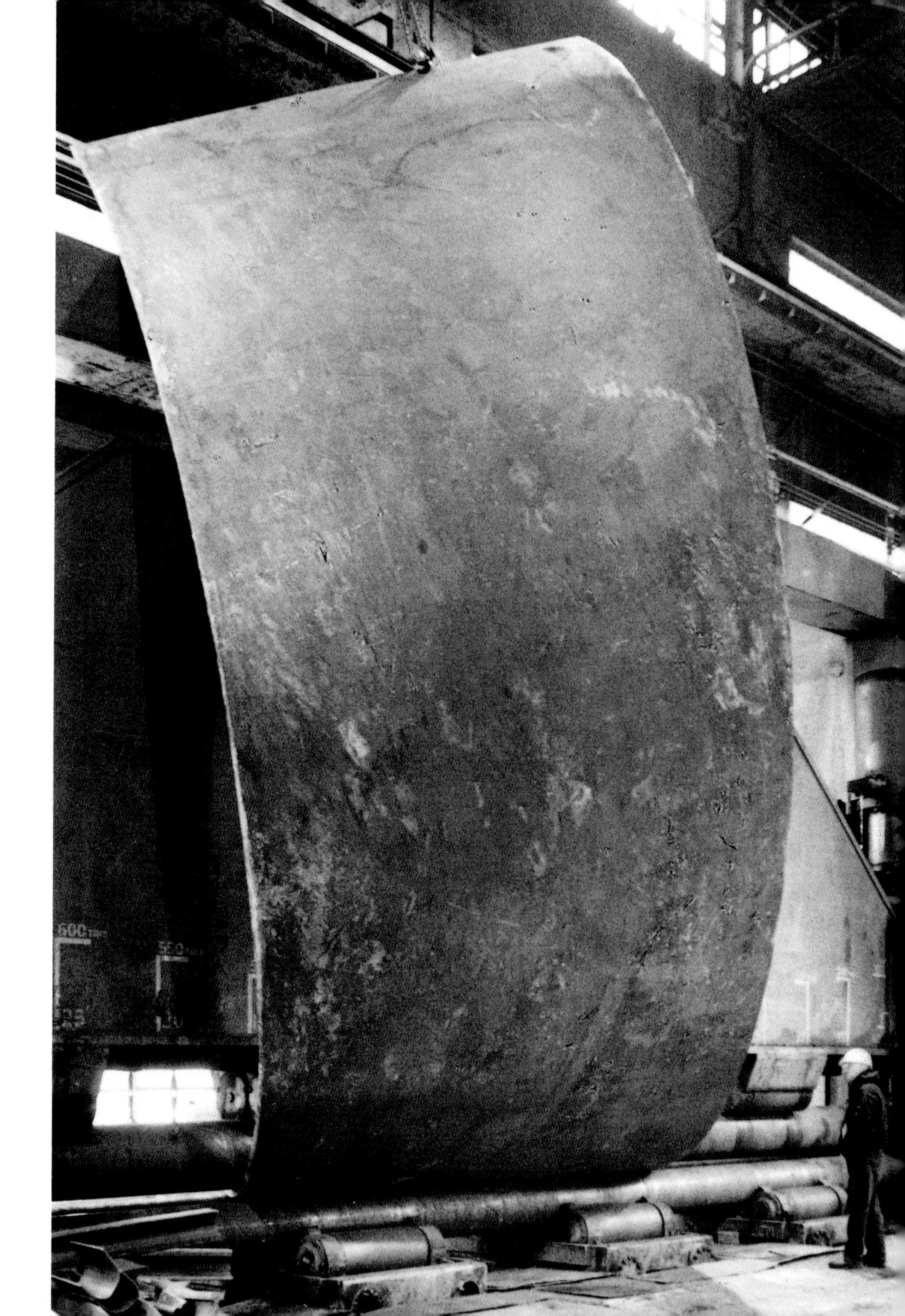

Staff
Michael Govan
Director
Barbara Clausen
Curatorial Assistant
Lynne Cooke
Curator
Stephen Dewhurst
Assistant Director
Steven Evans
Security & Visitor Services
Laura Fields
Finance/Graphics
Evonne Gallardo
Development Coordinator
Karen J. Kelly
Director of Publications and Special Programs
Michelle Marozik
Book Sales Manager
Brighde Mullins
Consulting Director of Poetry Series
Scott Myers
Education Coordinator
James Schaeufele
Director of Operations
Sara Schnittjer Tucker
Director of Digital Media
Alan Yamahata
Executive Assistant

Dia Art Council*
Plácido Arango
Janet and Gilbert de Botton
Frances and John Bowes
Sandra J. Brant
Constance R. Caplan
Donatella and Jay Chiat
Jan Cowles
Douglas S. Cramer
Frances and Thomas H. Dittmer
Valerie and John C. Evans
Doris and Donald G. Fisher
Saul A. Fox
Helyn and Ralph I. Goldenberg
Cathy and Stephen Graham
Ray A. Graham III
Nancy and Steven Grand-Jean
Anthony Grant
Mimi and Peter Haas
Frederick B. Henry
Jane Hertzmark
Marieluise Hessel
Tom Healy and Fred Hochberg
Elizabeth and Sidney Kahn
Simone and Paulo Klabin
Wanda M. Klabin
Wynn Kramarsky
Emily Fisher Landau
Anne and Patrick Lannan
Gretchen and Howard H. Leach
Ann Tenenbaum and Thomas H. Lee
Linda and Harry Macklowe
Eileen and Peter Norton
Nancy and Steven H. Oliver
Linda Pace
Giovanna and Giuseppe Panza di Biumo
Miuccia Prada and Patrizio Bertelli
Emily Rauh Pulitzer
Leanne and George R. Roberts
Kathy and Keith Sachs
Hannelore and Rudolph Schulhof
Helen and Charles R. Schwab
Lea H. Simonds
Charles Simonyi
Emily and Jerry Spiegel
Dorie and Paul Sternberg
Norah and Norman Stone
Susy and Jack Wadsworth
Nancy Brown Wellin
Pat and Bill Wilson
Barbara and Charles B. Wright
Virginia and Bagley Wright

**The Dia Art Council is Dia's major annual support group.*